PRAISE FOR

GOD'S SECRET TO GREATNESS

God's Secret to Greatness is must reading for every believer, but especially for those who are called to lead, for those who lead must be servant of all.

CHÉ AHN
SENIOR PASTOR, HARVEST ROCK CHURCH, PASADENA, CA

This book gets to the core of the ministry of Christ and of those who carried the gospel around the world.

GERALD COATES
SPEAKER, AUTHOR AND BROADCASTER

One of the truly great books of spiritual depth of the past 50 years. Poignant and gripping, *God's Secret to Greatness* is destined to change your life.

JOY DAWSON
INTERNATIONAL BIBLE TEACHER AND AUTHOR

David Cape and I have served together in leadership for 15 years. Now you will catch a wonderful picture of the servant heart and life I know so well. This book is not theory but, rather, a lifestyle that is contagious.

TONY FITZGERALD
TEAM LEADER, CHURCH OF THE NATIONS INTERNATIONAL

This book is an expression of its message—two notable ministers of God serving each other to produce a remarkable challenge to servanthood.

ROGER T. FORSTER
SENIOR PASTOR, ICHTHUS CHRISTIAN FELLOWSHIP, LONDON

A book that explains in dramatic detail no less than its title suggests.

TED HAGGARD
SENIOR PASTOR, NEW LIFE CHURCH, COLORADO SPRINGS, CO

Tommy Tenney and David Cape show us that humility is produced when our center is turned from self to God, allowing us to walk in true servanthood.

JANE HANSEN
PRESIDENT, AGLOW INTERNATIONAL

Opening the pages of this book will mark you for life. Its imprint on your soul will change the way you see the lost around you.

CINDY JACOBS
COFOUNDER, GENERALS OF INTERCESSION

Tommy Tenney has the unique gift to put into words what so many in the Body of Christ are feeling. *God's Secret to Greatness* is a masterpiece.

JOHN A. KILPATRICK,
SENIOR PASTOR, BROWNSVILLE ASSEMBLY OF GOD, PENSACOLA, FL

Reading this book will inform you; practicing its message will transform you.

DAVID RAVENHILL
AUTHOR OF *FOR GOD'S SAKE, GROW UP*

Tommy Tenney's prolific pen is igniting new flames of fervor and revival around the world.

SERGIO SCATAGLINI
AUTHOR OF *THE FIRE OF HIS HOLINESS*

GOD'S
SECRET TO
GREATNESS

THE POWER OF THE TOWEL

DAVID CAPE & TOMMY TENNEY

Regal

A Division of Gospel Light
Ventura, California, U.S.A.

Published by Regal Books
A Division of Gospel Light
Ventura, California, U.S.A.
Printed in the U.S.A.

Cover and Interior Design by Rob Williams
Edited by Larry Walker
Cover Photography by Chrisopher Zsarnay, Z Studios

Library of Congress Cataloging-in-Publication Data
Tenney, Tommy, 1956-
    God's secret to greatness / Tommy Tenney and David Cape.
        p. cm.
    Includes bibliographical references.
    ISBN 0-8307-2587-3
    1. Service (Theology) I. Title.

BT738.4 T46 2000
253—dc21   00-055252

  2 3 4 5 6 7 8 9 10 11 12 13 14 15 / 09 08 07 06 05 04 03 02 01 00

Rights for publishing this book in other languages are contracted by Gospel Literature International (GLINT). GLINT also provides technical help for the adaptation, translation and publishing of Bible study resources and books in scores of languages worldwide. For further information, contact GLINT, P.O. Box 4060, Ontario, CA 91761-1003, U.S.A. You may also send e-mail to Glintint@aol.com, or visit their website at www.glint.org.

DEDICATION

Daily they "wash our feet" and "chase after God."
They don't ever seek the limelight and are not
often seen "up front."

Yet they are two of the greatest servants we know.
Without them our callings would not be a reality.
Their names are Jeanie and Carol, our beloved
wives, to whom we dedicate this book.

CONTENTS

Preface 9

Acknowledgment 11

Chapter 1 13
Using the Right Weapon in the Wrong Realm

Chapter 2 19
His Presence Must Produce Transformation

Chapter 3 33
The Spirit of Servanthood Is Caught, Not Taught

Chapter 4 49
Serving with Dignity and Delight

Chapter 5 67
Servanthood Is a Heart Attitude, Not an Aptitude

Chapter 6 83
Understanding the Power of Servanthood
and the Importance of Shining Shoes

Chapter 7 95
Seeing What Jesus Sees

Chapter 8 115
Listening with Your Eyes and Seeing with Your Ears

Chapter 9 129
Turning Disappointment into a God Appointment

Chapter 10 151
Serving with the Preparation of Anticipation

Chapter 11 165
Plugging the Leaks and Serving for a Lifetime

PREFACE

The Creator implanted an innate sense of servanthood in every cell of the human body. Although each cell of the body shares a common DNA, each one serves a specific purpose for the good of the whole. Some cells are grouped together where they combine their talents to serve the body with a specialized function as an organ (such as the liver, the eye, the heart and the brain). On a larger scale, every body organ is dependent on the "selfless service" of the other organs and cells. Without it, life ceases. We may not realize it as we should, but the Body of Christ operates with the same interdependence.

When we agreed that the Lord wanted us to work together to write this book on servanthood, we each came to the task with particular strengths and a deep appreciation for the strengths we saw in each other. We had to *serve one another* so that we could serve you through this book. You will see two very different styles of writing and two very different methodologies of ministry in every chapter. That is a good thing because it is a small picture of the way God chose to work through His "many-membered" body.

Both of us preach the Word of God, but we do it very differently from one another. Both of us pastored churches for several years but under very different circumstances. Each of us maintains a demanding itinerant ministry schedule but primarily on different sides of the globe. It took God to bring us together. It took the power of servanthood to blend our hearts and messages into one book with one purpose: to help you fulfill your destiny and discover *the secret to greatness* in the power of servanthood.

If we could ask you to do one thing, it would be this: When you complete this book, don't retire it to some dusty shelf somewhere. Allow the Holy Spirit to revolutionize your life with the power of servanthood and put into action the things we've shared from God's Word. Then pass along this book to others, so we can serve them as well.

Remember, there is power in servanthood. Part of its secret resides in the wisdom to know when to swing the sword of the Spirit and when to extend the towel of servanthood. This is the way of the Cross, the secret of the empty tomb and the crowning glory of the reigning King. Be blessed in your serving, in Jesus' name.

The Authors

ACKNOWLEDGMENT

We want to thank our friend and editor Larry Walker, who sat down with his canvas and created an articulate journalistic tapestry, blending our two unique callings to form that which glorifies and reflects our creator, God. Larry's tireless enthusiasm and excellence go beyond the call of duty.

USING THE RIGHT WEAPON
IN THE WRONG REALM

When Jesus said, "The violent take it by force," He was referring to the spiritual battle for the kingdom of God—not your neighbor's house or the soloist's position in the church choir! It's possible to have the right weapon and be on the wrong battlefield. Just as it was often common courtesy in parts of the Wild West for men to lay down their pistols at the door of a church or public meeting, we must learn to put aside our "swords" and pick up the towel of servanthood in the presence of fellow Christians and non-Christians alike. We can have the *right weapon* but use it in the *wrong realm* and lose the war in the process!

The Scriptures say that "the weapons of our warfare are not carnal but mighty in God for pulling down strongholds."[1] It is appropriate and proper for us to use mighty weapons to pull down a demonic stronghold. However, strong weapons used in an inappropriate environment become like the proverbial "bull in the china closet": they wreak havoc.

The weapon of choice in the heavenly realm is obviously "the sword of the Spirit,"[2] but the weapon of choice in the earthly realm is a towel. Both weapons are effective—but only when each is used in the right realm.

Christians often pick up the sword of the Lord, take a defensive position (perhaps even an offensive position) and swing in anger, fear or judgment—dismembering Christ's Body in the process. I wonder if we recall what Jesus said to his sometimes divisive disciples at the Last Supper—"in *remembrance* of me"![3] To swing the sword on Earth often dismembers and divides. To sling the towel on Earth often *"re-members"*! Servanthood puts back together what has been forced apart.

The words of the thief on the cross[4] remind me that at times we whack away at "lowly sinners" in the world as if to bring judgment to them early. He asked Jesus to *re-member* him. That thief wasn't asking Jesus to merely *think about* him when He got to heaven; he *wanted to be with Jesus*. If I could paraphrase his request, it would seem to me that the thief is saying *"reattach me; put me where I belong; make me a mem-*

ber." The biblical terminology for this re-membering process is "grafted in."[5] If He is the vine and we are the branches,[6] then we must be attached.

Our misuse of God's "two-edged sword" is similar to the way Peter swung his sword at the high priest's servant when Jesus was arrested in the garden of Gethsemane.[7] I feel that Peter didn't aim his blow just to cut off Malchus's ear. It is good that the high priest's servant ducked quickly. Had he ducked a split second later, the Lord could have worked an even greater miracle by reattaching the man's head instead of merely reattaching his right ear.[8]

GOD CONSTANTLY REPAIRS THE DAMAGE WE DO

When we indiscriminately swing swords in the earthly realm, God must constantly repair the damage we do. Conversely, it is folly to use the towel of servanthood against a dark power or principality in the heavenlies. In this place of spiritual battle, only the sword of God's Word and His name will do. As the battle in the wilderness raged, Jesus said to Satan, *"It is written."*[9] Those who attempt to use the towel in the heavenlies may find themselves under subjection to Satan. He quickly takes advantage of the ignorance of unproven warriors, for he does not fear a towel.

Weapons are tools of influence that often represent the authority of a far greater power. Whether it is a Roman soldier brandishing a sword or a twenty-first-century law enforcement officer flashing a gun, the mere display of potentially deadly force is often sufficient to solve situations with the lawless and rebellious.

Satan will often leave "on credit" when a Christian simply mentions Jesus' name. Why? Jesus gave us His name as a weapon of power in the heavenlies. In the arsenal of a knowledgeable believer, the name of Jesus can release heaven's myriads of angels at a moment's notice or release the very *Shekinah* glory of God on the scene. For this reason it strikes fear among the ranks of the dark powers and principalities.

It is very important that we learn this vital lesson: *Use no swords on Earth*; they slice and divide the Body of Christ. Swords are to be used against Satan and his minions only.

My understanding of servanthood comes from years of practical experience, but it doesn't begin to compare with the "practicum" that Dave Cape, my coauthor, experienced under God's guiding hand. When I first met Dave, his effervescent joy deeply impressed me. He always seemed to be happy, but he seemed to be happiest when sharing the stories of how he discovered the dignity and the delight of servanthood. His life teaches that your ability to express humility and bring unity is no greater than your servant heart.

EVANGELISM WITH A CROSS AND A FOOT-WASHING BOWL

Dave Cape's amazing story is woven throughout this book. God apprehended Dave in 1988 and called him to resign from a successful pastorate in Johannesburg, South Africa. In October of that year, he begin an unprecedented journey into servanthood evangelism with a cross and a foot-washing bowl that would take him to countless nations of the world. The journey began in Soweto, a city of 3 million black South Africans, during the height of the "troubles" and violence, before the fall of apartheid in South Africa. This was the time of the dreaded "necklace murders," when angry crowds placed gasoline-filled tires around the necks of their victims and set them on fire.

The secret to true authority on the earth is a towel, not a sword.

Within minutes of Dave's arrival in Soweto, gang members surrounded him on the street and demanded to know what he was doing there. Dave's gentle spirit and servant heart defused their hatred and he led each of the men to the Lord Jesus. One of the men became his first companion on the journey to discover the secret power of servanthood.

I am excited and blessed to have this man of God as my partner in this project. Our goal is to explain some poorly understood but vital principles about the weapons of our warfare.

The towel is God's weapon of choice on Earth. Though few suspect it, this weapon is a true source of divine influence here. Our own Master took up the towel and became the greatest leader the earth has ever known. The towel is a pliable tool of a servant, but the Lord refused to limit the towel to those who merely occupied the occupational station of a servant. He said to His disciples and future apostles of the Church, "He who is greatest among you shall be your servant."[10] Humility and the spirit of a servant will conquer more opposing forces on earth than arrogance and false authority.

THE SECRET POWER OF THE TOWEL

As misunderstood as it is, the secret to true authority on the earth is a towel and not a sword. It must become our primary weapon of choice for earthly foes as we reserve the sword for use against the principalities and powers operating through people.

Jesus never attacked the person; He dealt directly with the power behind the person. When Jesus said to Peter, "Get behind Me, Satan! You are an offense to Me, for you are not mindful of the things of God, but the things of men,"[11] He looked past Peter to address the true motivating source. Jesus swiftly swung the sword of God at Satan's lie, but He did not damage Peter.

The Lord's actions in the incident with Peter illustrate the verse in the book of Hebrews that says, "For the word of God is living and powerful, and sharper than any two-edged sword, piercing even to the division of soul and spirit, and of joints and marrow, and is a discerner of the thoughts and intents of the heart."[12]

Jesus never rebuked the sinner, but He was quick and cutting when it came to the spirit of hypocrisy operating through religious people. He was quick to rebuke the actions of the religious self-righteous, while we are quick to rebuke sinners. That is an example of using the sword of God's Word in the wrong realm. Jesus became a servant to sinners while standing as Lord and King over unclean spirits operating through human hosts. It is critical that we make that distinction.

People are not our enemies; God sent us to serve people just as our Lord served us. It is time for us to put our swords in their sheaths and pick up a towel. The towel is our Savior's symbol on Earth. He "made Himself of no reputation [stripped Himself], taking the form of a bond-servant, and coming in the likeness of men."[13] The Son of God girded Himself with a towel, washed the feet of His disciples and became the servant of all. That is our model and the source of true greatness.

If our Lord picked up the towel, perhaps it is time for us to do the same. If we want to see God's will be done in this realm as it is in the heavenlies, then we must strip ourselves of our religious pretension and humble ourselves. We must become servants to the needs of those around us. By joining the appropriate use of the servant's towel in the earthly realm with the use of the sword in the heavenly realm, we will see hell split wide open, dismember Satan's dark realm and wreck the very gates of hell while we *re-member* His Body!

Notes
1. 2 Corinthians 10:4.
2. Ephesians 6:17.
3. 1 Corinthians 11:24,25.
4. Luke 23:42, italics mine.
5. Romans 11:17-24.
6. See John 15:5.
7. Hebrews 4:12 ("two-edged sword"); see John 18:10 (Simon Peter is identified as the sword swinger in the garden).
8. See John 18:10; Luke 22:50,51.
9. Matthew 4:4, italics mine.
10. Matthew 23:11.
11. Matthew 16:23.
12. Hebrews 4:12.
13. Philippians 2:7.

HIS PRESENCE MUST PRODUCE TRANSFORMATION

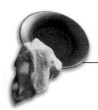

Millions of Christians around the world suffer from the apostle Peter's "rooftop syndrome." We become so absorbed in our "rooftop" worship experience that we don't want to leave it long enough to take Jesus' presence to the streets and into the world of the lost.

The book of Acts tells us that Peter the apostle received a heavenly vision on a rooftop in Joppa. While he sat on the roof and tried to figure out its meaning, the Holy Spirit told him, "Behold, *three men are seeking you*. Arise therefore, go down and go with them, doubting nothing; for I have sent them."[1]

God is determined to get the gospel (and the revelation of His presence) from the rooftop to the street. Untold numbers of unreached people live and work around our churches and beside us in the workplace. In the spirit realm, they knock on our doors and say, "We are hungry; we are hurting and destitute. Will somebody help us?" Too often we reply, "Excuse me, I'm having a vision." Like Peter, we forget that *the mission for the vision of God's presence is to take it to the street.*

When we don't allow God's presence to produce transformation and action, His message becomes meaningless. Peter evidently suffered serious relapses of his rooftop syndrome. He seemingly preferred experiencing the pleasant feelings and the public approval created by visionary experience to actually *doing* what the vision required. The apostle Paul publicly challenged Peter for clinging to the comfortable circles of his prejudiced religious friends rather than reaching beyond that closed circle to extend God's love to people that his church culture taught were unlovely.[2]

We do the same thing when we choose to exclusively focus on "worshiping" God while ignoring Christ's command to "go into all the world and preach the gospel to every creature."[3] In our eagerness to soak in more of His Spirit, we sidestep His commission to be Spirit-filled and empowered witnesses for Him "in Jerusalem, and in all Judea and Samaria, and to the end of the earth."[4] *God's highest purpose is not to grow churches but to gather worshipers.*

JESUS PULLED AWAY TO PRAY AND HE MINISTERED TO PEOPLE ALL DAY

No one loved and longed for the Father's presence more than Jesus did during His earthly journey. He prayed often, but He also demonstrated the fruits of His intimacy with His Father on a daily basis. He pulled away to pray and seek His Father's face, but then He walked right into the midst of hurting crowds of people day after day, even when He knew His enemies were waiting for Him.

Jesus couldn't ignore the crowds, although at times He had to pull away from them. He looked at hurting people as a loving shepherd surveys his flock.[5] It was as if He couldn't pass by a casket and a weeping mother without doing something about the problem.[6]

At times, Jesus purposely passed by the sick, but those instances were dictated by divine assignments that took precedence over the unending needs of the people around Him. This was the case when He healed the man lying by the Pool of Bethesda.[7] Jesus seemed to be motivated by the very compassion of God, as if the prodding presence of the Father moved and directed Him from within.

The gospel of Jesus Christ is a practical gospel that is as concerned with *doing* something as it is with *being* something. Good works won't get you into heaven, but once you receive new life from Jesus, He expects you to do what He did for the rest of your life. It comes with the territory. Godly people do godly things or they aren't godly.

SO YOU CAN'T PREACH—CAN YOU TEACH THREE-YEAR-OLDS ABOUT JESUS?

You may never raise someone from the dead, but you can comfort the sick. You may never be able to open blind eyes, but you can change the oil in a single mother's car or prepare a meal for your ill neighbor. You may not be called to preach on the street corner or declare God's Word before thousands, but you could teach a class of three-year-olds that Jesus loves them.

There is something about serving others that is near and dear to God's heart. Once you begin to serve "carryout" anointing to others, you might be surprised by God's response. In the middle of your service to others, you may well experience the miraculous! God's presence transformed Stephen from an anointed table waiter into an anointed miracle worker in the street![8]

I love and treasure the wonder of God's intimate presence, yet my original calling and passion as a soul-winning evangelist has never left my heart or my thoughts. One of my greatest desires is to see the Church take the transforming power of God's presence to the streets and cities of the world. As I noted in my book *God's Favorite House*, "We know what it looks like when God visits a church, but we've not yet seen what it looks like when He visits a city!"[9]

God has never been in love with buildings, and He despises anything that separates Him from intimate fellowship with the people He created. Most Christians are safely tucked away in the folds of hundreds of thousands of local churches. He is looking for people who will accept His commission to seek, serve and to save those who are lost. God wants us to venture beyond the four walls of our worship centers and steepled church buildings to take His light into the darkness and become His hands of mercy and love extended to those who do not know Him.

Dave Cape's amazing journey of servanthood sets the stage for virtually any examination of our high call to be servants.

THEY CROSSED THEIR NATION ARMED WITH A TOWEL, A CROSS AND A BOWL

As I mentioned in the first chapter, Dave was the pastor of a church in Johannesburg, South Africa, until the Lord spoke one word to him: *"servant."* In the process of working out the meaning and purpose of that single word, Dave and his wife, Carol, resigned their positions in the local church and began to walk the length of their nation armed with a towel and a cross with a wooden bowl attached where the two crossmembers joined together.

Dave carried the cross and bowl on foot while Carol and their children followed behind in a vehicle (where possible). His mission (which still continues somewhere in the world at this writing) was to wash the feet of everyone he possibly could on that journey.

He began in northeastern South Africa, at the perimeter of Soweto, the violence-prone city southwest of Johannesburg. Then he washed feet and experienced countless miracles all along the way to Cape Town, in the extreme southwestern region of South Africa. His journey would be similar to walking from New York to Los Angeles on foot while carrying approximately 45 pounds of equipment and water on your back.

The idea of approaching strangers with a request to wash their feet sounds strange and uncomfortable to most of us, but Dave Cape has a disarming ability to persuade prostitutes, presidents and paupers to put their feet in his wooden foot-washing bowl. Perhaps his secret lies in the many tears that are mingled with the water in that bowl.

WOULD YOU WASH THE FEET OF STRANGERS?

The Capes dared to obey God's unorthodox call to a supernatural servanthood ministry, and they touched entire cities with the compassion of God. Their obedient service helped to change their nation and birthed a powerful international ministry. Best of all, these miracles did not spring from the premise of a pulpit; they were birthed over a bowl and with a towel as Dave knelt and washed the feet of strangers on hot, dusty roads.

It is not as important that we preach the message of God's love as it is that we live and do it.

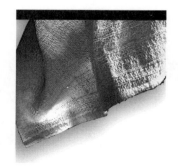

Dave and I decided to work together and blend my heart with his insights drawn from more than a decade of washing feet and ministering in the Word on many continents. His stories, sermons and messages are never thundered from a pulpit as a three-point sermon on how we must serve. He shares with sinners and saints alike with the same compassion that compels him to walk the roads of many nations and kneel behind the bowl in service. He washes the feet and souls of others, although his own feet ache and his hands are fouled with the debris he washes into his bowl.

That simple act involves more than mere water and a towel. This service of servanthood is endued with power from on high. The compassion, mercy and grace of God bathe the feet and souls of those Dave serves. The power of the Holy Spirit flows through the hands of His servant to wash away the rejection, pain and hurt from every weary traveler he meets.

This is our point: It is not as important that we *preach* the message of God's love as it is that we *live and do* it. I have been told that St. Francis of Assisi said, "Preach always—if necessary use words."[10]

Dave and Carol Cape discovered at the end of their journey from Soweto to Cape Town that God had more for them to do. Dave found himself carrying his cross and bowl and washing feet from Kurdistan to Iraq in the middle of the Gulf War. Once again, God supernaturally protected him and demonstrated the power of servanthood to people on both sides of the battle line—whether they were Muslim, Christian or Jewish. God's compassion also led him to the parched land of Sudan where millions of people hovered between life and death due to chronic drought, perpetual starvation, and continuous warfare between competing forces.

One of the most difficult places Dave encountered on his journey with the cross and bowl was in the United States along the Pacific coastline of sunny California. Here, more than in any other place, he knew that God's presence had to demonstrate transformation and power to overcome the countless distractions of a culture steeped in the pursuit of self-satisfaction.

DAVID   SPEAKS

Carol and I faced one of our greatest challenges when we received a clear word from God to carry the cross and bowl northward along the

California coast. We knew the mission would be lengthy and that it would demand a tremendous investment of finances and faith, but we had no idea just how difficult it would be.

We endured weeks of spiritual attack as we prepared for the trip, but finally I stepped onto the side of the road near the Mexican border close to San Diego, California. We had just enough money to stay in a trailer park for one week (if we didn't spend any money on food).

WE ENCOUNTERED EVERY KIND OF ISM YOU COULD IMAGINE

We didn't realize we would face one of the most difficult testing times in more than a decade of ministry on the road. We encountered every kind of ism you could imagine, including humanism, feminism, socialism and materialism, along with assertive homosexuality and every other type of deviancy motivated by evil spirits. I was to meet more whackos walking up that coastline than I had met in any of my other travels!

We faced constant challenges without a single ministry breakthrough for almost two months. (Carol and I have found that dry periods like that often seem worse than the openly demonic threats we face in our ministry.) We visited very few churches, and finances remained impossibly tight. One day Carol cried out in desperation as I walked away from the truck with the cross and bowl. With tears streaming down her cheeks, she said, "God, please do something!"

On the first day of July, I found myself in the bustling resort of Laguna Beach. It was jam-packed with a maze of barely clothed but well-oiled and tanned bodies, and I looked on the scene in amazement. Everyone in sight was dressed for the beach and I felt like an odd jungle explorer with my hiking shoes, road gear and cross and bowl.

I silently prayed, *God, would it ever be possible for You to do anything here?* Then I saw a surfer emerge from the water, sporting long hair, a ring in his ear and a body covered with tattoos. He glanced at me through the crowd and gave me the thumbs-up sign. That was all the invitation I needed!

After I waded through the mass of humanity to reach the surfer, I explained what I was doing. He just shook his head and said, "All this Jesus stuff, man—it can't work for me." When I asked what he meant, he just showed me his arm. It was black and blue from the countless times he had injected drugs into his veins. He admitted that he was a chronic drug addict. I said, "Jesus can set you free right now." Then I shared the message of the gospel and told him Jesus had come to set him free.

MY TATTOOED FRIEND SURRENDERED HIS HEART AND PUT HIS FEET IN THE BOWL

By a sovereign act of God, I found myself kneeling on the hot sands of Laguna Beach with a drug addict I had met only minutes earlier. In full view of everyone, my tattooed friend surrendered his heart to Jesus and put his feet in my bowl mounted on a wooden cross. He was still dripping wet from the surf as I washed his feet and cast the bondage of drug abuse from him in Jesus' name. By this time, we had the attention of nearly everyone on the beach. Before we had finished, another man said, "Yes, me too!" and I began to wash his feet as he surrendered his heart to Jesus. Then there was a third . . .

Early that afternoon, I met a young man who was part of an informal beach community at Laguna Beach. He introduced me to several other young men and women who simply camped out on the beach and lived on whatever food they could find. When I learned that they hadn't eaten much in recent days, I promised to return that night with food (by faith, of course).

I returned to the trailer and rejoiced with Carol over the things God had done, and then I told her about my promise to feed the beach dwellers that night. She took what little money we had left to buy several loaves of bread and spent the rest of the afternoon making piles of sandwiches. "What happens if they don't show up tonight?" she asked. I could only answer, "I suppose we'll be eating sandwiches for the next few weeks!"

When Carol and I returned to the beach that evening, my new friends showed up along with a whole new group of friends. After we fed them, we prayed and shared the love of Jesus with each of them. We realized that as we had been blessed by God's presence that afternoon, His manifest presence now was opening the way for loving deeds of service that night. What we didn't know, however, was that God's work that day had also released the trigger that would catapult us into such a frenzy of fervor and ministry over the next few months that we would barely be able to cope with it.

GOD SAID THIS WAS MY LAST CHANCE

The following week, the Lord led us to a group of 30 ex-convicts, drug addicts and prostitutes. I had the privilege of sharing the gospel with them and told them how precious they were to Jesus. In Him, they had a future and a hope regardless of what was in their past. We led eight of them to the Lord and baptized them immediately. I asked each one to share briefly before I dunked them, and one man said, "I got out of jail just yesterday and I figured that God said this was my last chance. I want all that He has for my life."

We weren't in a church service or a house of worship (although we dearly love both), but we were walking and dwelling in God's presence nonetheless. In addition, we could see the power of His presence being transformed into divine action. The Christian life never can be only works any more than it can be only presence. The two must be balanced in our lives to reflect the glory of the Creator.

YOU CANNOT DWELL IN GOD'S PRESENCE AND REMAIN UNCHANGED

The Bride of Christ, the Church, has experienced many outpourings of the Holy Spirit and divine visitations in recent years. We should count it a privilege to be alive during such an exciting time, but we have a serious problem that must be corrected. Far too many Christians believe they can dwell in God's presence and remain unchanged in their lifestyles and their unwillingness to serve in God's kingdom.

God disagrees. He exhorted us through James the apostle, "Be doers of the word, and not hearers only, deceiving yourselves."[11] People have good reason to doubt the genuineness of your faith if you say, "I have been in God's presence," but it fails to transform your life or theirs.

Several years ago, Carol and I took a man into our home after his life and marriage were destroyed by an ungodly lifestyle and a series of wrong choices. He traveled 700 miles to reach our home, and when he arrived, all of his earthly possessions barely filled the backseat of his rented car.

Carol and I agreed before his arrival that we would stand with him as he set out to restore his life. We also set four prayer goals for his life: We wanted to see him restored spiritually, financially, socially and domestically.

Our friend began his journey to wholeness that very next morning, which was a Sunday, by making his life right with Jesus at the altar of our home church. At that point, we eagerly waited and watched to see if the seed God planted in his heart would genuinely take root. It did.

The world must see a difference in the lives of those who claim to have been in God's presence.

He enrolled in the new-members class and joined the church soon afterwards. Then he completed a divorce recovery program *twice* and began to develop caring friendships with godly, loving people in the church (earlier in his life, he always seemed to pick friends who took him further from the Lord).

He landed an excellent job and began to repay his debts and reestablish himself financially. Within a matter of months, he was able to move to his own apartment, although Carol and I continued to see him almost daily when we weren't ministering somewhere.

TRANSFORMED IN THE PRESENCE OF THE LORD

Slowly but surely, our friend began to blossom as he spent more time in the presence of the Lord. At this writing, he has celebrated his first anniversary of marriage to a fine lady from our local church body (I had the privilege of conducting the wedding service). All four goals we set for our friend in prayer were achieved because *his life in the presence of the Lord transformed him.*

The world *must see a difference* in the lives of those who claim to have been in God's presence. There is no exception to this truth in the Scriptures or in the history of the Church.

When Moses, the murderer on the run, turned aside from the usual sheep path to investigate the burning bush on Mount Horeb, he encountered the presence of the living God and it changed him!

God always reveals Himself to us for a divine purpose; He is not interested in merely thrilling or entertaining us. God explained to Moses what was going on with the Israelites in Egypt, and then He said, *"Come now,* therefore, and *I will send you* to Pharaoh that you may bring My people, the children of Israel, out of Egypt."[12]

Moses did not return the same way he came. He was permanently and unalterably changed by his encounter with the living God. His life turned a corner in the presence of God and there would be no turning back. He obediently returned to Egypt as a transformed man, and his obedience led to the miraculous emancipation of his entire nation from Egypt's bondage.

MOSES' FACE REFLECTED THE GLORY OF GOD'S PRESENCE

Later on, Moses' life demonstrated a *divine difference* in another way that affected everyone who saw him. When he descended from Mount Sinai with the Ten Commandments, after spending 40 days with God, the Scriptures say that "Moses did not know that the skin of his face shone while he talked with Him."[13] Moses' face literally *reflected the glory of God's presence.* He actually had to put a veil over his face before the Israelites could bear to look at him! (If that happened to us after an encounter with the Lord, our faces would probably appear on every television news program on the planet.)

If you have been with the Lord, you will reflect Him. God's presence has transforming power that cannot and will not leave a human life unchanged. Saul of Tarsus was the most notorious hunter of Christians in the New Testament—until the day he encountered the living God on the road to Damascus.

God's presence so transformed this zealous "seminary-trained" rabbi that Saul the persecutor instantly became Paul the believer. Here are the results of a single *transforming encounter with the presence of God:*

- one of the Church's greatest apostles;
- the evangelization of all of Asia in only two years;
- a rich legacy of wisdom from Paul's ministry in the form of his written epistles to the Church, comprising the majority of the New Testament Scriptures.

GOD STILL DESIRES THAT ALL MEN BE SAVED

God's presence is something to be enjoyed, savored, cherished and honored; but it must never be hoarded, reserved or held for an elite few. We serve a God "who desires all men to be saved and to come to the knowledge of the truth."[14] That fact hasn't changed. Those who actually spend time in the presence of the Lord leave with a strong sense of love and forgiveness for others combined with a burning compassion for the lost.

His presence also gives us something that cannot be found in any other place. The Bible says, "In Your presence is fullness of joy."[15] It also says, "Repent therefore and be converted, that your sins may be blotted out, so that times of refreshing may come from the presence of the Lord."[16]

Supernatural joy and refreshing have nothing to do with circumstances or our personal efforts. They are both gifts from God and visible evidence that we have been in the Lord's presence. These two godly characteristics can be mimicked and imitated for a time, but the imitation quickly falls away when the pressures of servanthood and faithfulness in a fallen world begin to mount. No matter how difficult the going gets, the real thing acquired in God's presence never fades or falters. God's joy rises up even in the midst of our human despair or sadness. His refreshing sweeps in like a sudden spring rain on a hot day, pushing aside everything in its path. These are the treasures we should glean from the time we spend in His presence.

Did you notice there is a condition attached to our entrance into God's presence? We must enter His presence with repentance before we can receive the benefit of His refreshing.

YOU CAN'T LEAD PEOPLE WHERE YOU HAVEN'T GONE

I often tell pastors, "You cannot take your people where you have not been, nor can you lead them into what you have not personally experienced." The same principle applies in our ministry of joy and refreshing to others. There is no substitute for spending time in the presence of the Lord, and the presence of God should always produce transformation.

The presence of the Lord also affects people in another way that is obvious and unusual. I've noticed that God's presence often releases a spirit of giving in our hearts that is difficult to explain. It is nothing less than a miraculous transformation. (Many of us have a tighter grip on our wallet than anything else in our lives!)

The Lord released a spirit of giving during a meeting I attended, after a minister stood up to receive an offering and began to share the scriptural truth that God gives seed to the *sower*.[17] The minister asked the congregation how many of them genuinely wanted to give into the offering but did not have any seed to sow. When about 100 people in the auditorium raised their hands, he pulled a stack of folded ten- and twenty-dollar bills from his pocket and asked the people to come forward.

As the people began to stream forward, a *spirit of giving broke out* spontaneously among the people. Many of them began to approach others in the congregation and say, "The Lord told me to bless you with a gift."

When the preacher finally ran out of seed money, people in the congregation began to hand out money to those who had none so that everyone in the congregation could experience the joy of sowing into God's principles.

When the offering was finally received, the congregation gave a total of $65,000 that evening. I am convinced the power of God was released that evening because of what happened *before* the offering was received; the people who were there entered into an extended time of sweet worship and honored Him as the most important guest of all. We all lingered in His sweet presence that night.

In my mind, this is yet another experience that proves you cannot be in His presence without being fundamentally transformed and changed in a way that shows. Much of the time that transformation reveals itself in the way you view and serve others. *If you have been with Him, you reflect Him.*

Notes
1. Acts 10:19,20, italics mine.
2. See Galatians 2:11-21.
3. Mark 16:15.
4. Acts 1:8.
5. See Matthew 9:36.
6. See Luke 7:11-15.
7. See John 5:2-9.
8. See Acts 6:2-6,8.
9. Tommy Tenney, *God's Favorite House* (Shippensburg, PA: Destiny Image Publishers, Fresh Bread Publishing, 1999), p. 123.
10. Many have attributed this quote to St. Francis of Assisi, but as of this writing I have not found an original written source or citation.
11. James 1:22.
12. Exodus 3:10, italics mine.
13. Exodus 34:29.
14. 1 Timothy 2:4.
15. Psalm 16:11; see also Psalm 21:6.
16. Acts 3:19.
17. See 2 Corinthians 9:10.

CHAPTER THREE

THE SPIRIT OF SERVANTHOOD IS CAUGHT, NOT TAUGHT

The spirit of servanthood makes the difference between duty and desire, between doing what you have to do and doing what you want to do. Servanthood becomes a delight when you draw so close to the Lord that His desires become your desires. Only then will doing the will of God cease to be a duty. The load may be heavy at times, but it will always be lighter when you carry it with desire and delight.

If I went shopping while carrying your child in my arms, I have to admit that I would probably get tired. On the other hand, if I carried my own child on that trip, I promise you that my strength would stretch to new limits. It isn't necessarily because one child is lighter than the other. The difference rests in the fact that carrying my child is not just a duty to me; it is my heart's desire because that's my baby.

It is easy to forget that Jesus Christ asked us to do more than take up our crosses.[1] He also said, "Whoever compels you to go one mile, go with him two."[2] It is no small thing to step under the yoke of servanthood with Jesus,[3] but it can be nearly unbearable if you approach it as just your duty.

Yes, you may manage to do what you have to do; but I can guarantee that you will never *become all that you can be* until you move beyond mere duty and into the arena of desire. *The zeal and passion of humble servanthood is better caught than taught.*

You can't teach or model humility if it is not in your heart; it is a heart issue. Have you noticed how easy it is to pick out the pretenders in a crowd? The physical pretense of acting out humility comes across as a saccharin-sweet facade. It is artificial to the core, and artificial sweeteners are known for leaving a bitter aftertaste. Frankly, the world and the Church are tired of the bitter aftertaste left by people who act like they are something they are not. It is time for the Church to stop pretending and start becoming.

ZEAL IS PURPOSE ON FIRE

One of the most important keys to success in God's kingdom is zeal. This means *purpose on fire*. Often, it is conspicuously missing from the

Church. Zeal can only be birthed from passion, and passion is also better caught than taught. Before you can burn for God, you must catch the fire of His heart. When you fall in love with the One who made you, the passion of love propels you into a whole new world of giving service and willing sacrifice. Life becomes an eternal race to *outgive* God (a race you are destined to lose for eternity).

When the passion and zeal of love overtake you, life takes on a purpose that makes you think nothing of working long hours each day while serving others. Serving others and worshiping the Father become your burning mission in this life, just as they became so for Jesus.

Immediately after Jesus drove the moneychangers out of the Temple with a whip, His disciples remembered the prophecy in the Psalms: "Zeal for Your house has eaten Me up."[4] Jesus "caught the disease" of zeal for His Father's house and it was like cancer that was eating Him up. God isn't afraid of passion—*He invented it!*

Once we catch the fire of the Lord's servant heart, we become incurable servants. Even if we accept a position of leadership or authority over others, we tend to lead by example rather than by word only. We are the first ones to wait on tables and serve others because we know instinctively that no one in God's kingdom graduates from the ministry of helps[5] or the school of servant-hood. When the flame of servanthood ignites, we can never become so accustomed to a leadership position that we forget we were born to be servants after the example of our Master.

> *Once we catch the fire of the Lord's servant heart, we become incurable servants.*

PASSIONATE SERVANTHOOD

Dave and his wife, Carol, are consumed with servanthood. The Capes can't help themselves; they are passionate about the mission God gave them. Servanthood is a divine lifestyle they will follow all the days of their lives. We have much to learn from their example.

Servants habitually care more for the feelings of others than for their own. Our first allegiance as servants of God is to our Lord and Master. His concerns and wishes must come first before our own desires and before the needs and wants of others. Once we know we are walking in the Master's will, we can focus on those whom God sends us to serve.

Servants bless, even when those they serve curse and misuse them. Anyone who works in what the secular world calls the service industry can tell you that people are their biggest problem. People can be rude, uncaring, callous or incredibly cruel at times. This is especially true when we approach them with the good news of Jesus Christ.

Nevertheless, Jesus said, "I tell you not to resist an evil person. But whoever slaps you on your right cheek, turn the other to him also."[6] Why did He say such a thing? He said this because He knew we would have to abdicate our rights in order to become servants. However, a unique thing happens when you enter servanthood because of your passion for the Master. Once you settle the matter and accept the fact that in Christ you have no rights, from that moment on, you are freed of carrying the responsibility for your future. Your life is no longer your own; it is in your Master's hands.[7] The good news is that the Master can care for your future better than you can.

DAVID SPEAKS

I appreciate Tommy Tenney's kind words about the ministry God gave Carol and me, but I must admit that it took a pointed word from God to shake me out of my comfortable routine. We answered the call and have washed thousands upon thousands of feet in the Lord's name over the last decade or so; yet *it is nothing* if we fail to approach the *next* set of dirty feet with a genuine spirit of humility and servant-hood.

GREATNESS IN GOD'S EYES

Have you noticed that when God's Word speaks of men becoming great, it does so in terms that defy our normal thinking patterns and assumptions about leadership? Jesus told His bickering disciples:

> Whoever desires to become **great** among you, let him be your **servant.** And whoever desires to be first among you, let him be your slave—just as the Son of Man did not come to be served, but to serve, and to give His life a ransom for many.[8]

Most of us nod our heads and even preach this truth to others, but too few of us ever live it out in real life. I believe that most people never break through into the realm of servanthood because they haven't *caught* the passionate spirit of the One who came to serve. Those who do, begin to take on some or all of the biblical characteristics of true servants in God's kingdom.

Five Characteristics of Every True Servant

1. Servants must be prepared to humble themselves.

God has always been more interested in what is on the inside than what is on the outside of a person. When I think of true servants, I often think of the late Mother Teresa, the humble Catholic nun who devoted her life to serving the poor, the destitute and the dying in India's crowded cities.

Mother Teresa wouldn't have made it through even one Hollywood screen test. In terms of famous faces or superficially beautiful smiles, she wouldn't have even come close. Yet every world leader, celebrity and power broker on Earth wanted to shake her hand or spend time with her. In her final years she barely weighed 70 pounds and her bent frame made it appear as if she were composed mostly of skin and bones. Yet none of these things mattered in the sight of God. He was interested in the way her passion for Christ touched the lives of millions of hurting people over decades of dedicated service to the poorest of the poor and to India's "untouchables." God was only interested in her heart.

This reminds me of the time God chose a ruddy-faced shepherd boy who was small in stature. The day would come when this boy would stand between two armies and defy the enemies of God even as he was dwarfed by the eclipse of Goliath's shadow.

Young David was just a shepherd with a servant heart, the youngest of eight brothers, who was mocked by his older and bigger siblings. Yet God chose David over his brothers because he had a God-sized heart wrapped in a small body. The Lord knew the measure of David's heart long before David faced Goliath.

Israel's first king, Saul, chose to please man more than God and disqualified himself as the leader of God's people. That was when the Lord sent Samuel the prophet to anoint one of the sons of Jesse as king. Samuel thought he had a winner when he saw Jesse's handsome eldest son, Eliab, but God interrupted him and said, "Do not look at his appearance or at his physical stature, because I have refused him. For the LORD does not see as man sees; for *man looks at the outward appearance, but the LORD looks at the heart.*"[9]

God rejected each of the seven sons that Samuel examined, and when the prophet questioned Jesse, he learned there was an eighth son tending his father's sheep. Samuel refused to sit down until Jesse brought his forgotten son back from the fields. The Bible says, "Then Samuel took the horn of oil and anointed him *in the midst of his brothers;* and the Spirit of the LORD came upon David from that day forward."[10]

Meanwhile, the Spirit of the Lord *departed* from Saul and an evil spirit began to plague him. At the urging of his servants, King Saul sent a message to Jesse: "Send me your son David, *who is with the sheep.*"[11] The Bible says that Saul loved David greatly at that time and made him his armor bearer.[12]

David returned to feed his father's sheep for a time and King Saul focused on his problems with the Philistines. Then David took supplies to his older brothers at the battlefront and overheard Goliath defy the armies of Israel. He quickly found himself in King Saul's field quarters being fitted with the same armor he cared for when he wasn't home with the sheep! But David chose to battle Goliath with the shepherd's tools he had used against the lion and the bear that tried to ravage his father's flock. Goliath took the fall, and the army of Israel finished the job.

Once again, David found favor in Saul's eyes; but the goodwill would soon end. After the king made David a commander over his army, Saul overheard the women of Israel singing better songs about David than about him, and a murderous spirit of jealousy settled into his heart. He tried to kill David seven times in five different ways before David finally fled for his life.[13]

David didn't enter King Saul's courts bragging that Samuel had anointed him as Saul's replacement. He entered as a servant and was entrusted with the king's armor—a highly trusted position.

Saul's paranoid fears that David wanted to steal his kingdom mounted day by day. Yet even when Saul's anger burned him, David dodged the spears but refused to sling them back. He continued to love and respect King Saul, even after the king forced him into exile. Why? Because he had developed the humble heart of a servant. Somehow God always brings us back to the things of the heart.

When Carol and I served as pastors of a church in South Africa, we decided to provide hot tea to the congregation on Sunday mornings after the service (this is a popular custom in our nation). We quickly discovered that everyone wanted to drink tea, but no one wanted to wash the cups. Since the church did not have an automatic dishwasher, we had a logistical problem on our hands. Then the Lord challenged us and said, "If you want the members of the church to wash the cups, then *you* must wash the cups first!"

The Lord wants us to be willing to do whatever we ask others to do.

Fellowship was our primary goal, and if it cost us the labor of washing dishes on Sunday mornings, so be it. While everyone else fellowshipped and enjoyed their tea and cake, Carol and I slipped into the kitchen to wash several hundred cups. The same thing happened the following week, but this time a lady entered the kitchen

and exclaimed, "Oh, you're washing the cups!" We just smiled and said, "Sure, we're having fun." (We sang and praised God while we worked.)

She disappeared and quickly returned with a friend to join us in our kitchen praisefest. The following week, our two helpers returned with two more and they all helped us praise the Lord and wash the cups. The following week, we couldn't even squeeze into the kitchen to help wash the cups. The jobs were taken and we knew we had passed another small test from the Lord. I don't want this to sound super-spiritual; we simply did what the Lord had asked us to do and other people "caught" it too. The Lord wants us to be willing to do whatever we ask others to do.

Sometimes God requires us to humble ourselves in the line of duty. During my second year on the road, God instructed me to walk into a "bad" part of a city and wash feet on the streets. I felt that by that time I had already forsaken all for Christ. I assumed that my fleshly man was reasonably dead, but God was going to make sure of it.

One evening I came to a rundown part of the city at rush hour when the lines for the city buses were long and several rows deep. It was the perfect place for an evangelist to have a captive audience. The commuters would lose their place in line if they left, so they had to listen.

Hundreds of people pressed close to the edge of the sidewalk, packed shoulder to shoulder in hopes of making the next bus. As I ministered to one lady, the Lord really began to touch her. She couldn't step back or sit down because there was another line behind her and a third line behind that. Then I sensed the Lord was saying to me, "Wash her feet."

There was no room to spare on the packed sidewalk; the only clear area available to me was the gutter. The only problem was the filthy green slime flowing there. I thought, *O God, where are we going to go?* He instantly responded: "Tell her to sit where she is; you can kneel in the gutter and wash her feet."

I had my answer, so I knelt down in the slimy filth of the gutter with all the stinking muck flowing around my knees and washed that precious woman's feet. Meanwhile hundreds of people temporarily forgot their anxious concerns about catching a bus. When I finished, the Lord seemed to say to me, "I just wanted to see how much you are prepared to do." The Lord constantly reminds us that a servant must always be pre-pared to humble himself.

2. Servants must be zealous.

By Tommy's definition, zeal is "purpose on fire." King David of the Bible perfectly illustrates what Tommy was talking about. The first thing David did in Hebron when the people of Israel named him their king was to organize a national homecoming for the Ark of the Covenant.[14] Unfortunately, David first attempted to transport the Ark by using a new cart drawn by oxen according to the Philistine method. When the cart became unstable at Chidon's threshing floor, a young man named Uzzah presumptuously touched the Ark and God instantly struck him down.[15]

David returned to Jerusalem and then decided to try a second time, using consecrated Levite priests to transport the Ark of the Presence on their shoulders. This time the results were very different. Thirty-five thousand people accompanied David on the journey to bring the Ark to Jerusalem. The inference is that every six paces the entire caravan would stop while the priests offered a sacrifice to God, and everyone danced before the Lord.

By the time King David's joyous caravan reached Jerusalem, David's zeal for God's presence burned at full strength. The Bible says, "Then David danced before the LORD with all his might; and David was wear-ing a linen ephod."[16]

Eventually, David stripped down to his underwear in uninhibited wor-ship and praise to God. (I encourage you to get excited about the Lord, but I don't suggest that you go this far!) The point is that we serve a passion-ate God who delights in our zeal and passion for Him and His kingdom.

In his classic book *The God Chasers*, Tommy described a new zeal and passion that can transform the Church as we know it:

> Since we don't want to be too radical, we line all the chairs up in
> nice rows and expect our services to conform to equally straight
> and regimented lines as well. We need to get so desperately hun-
> gry for Him *that we literally forget our manners!* . . .

Everybody whom I can think of in the New Testament record who "forgot their manners" received something from Him. I'm not talking about rudeness for the sake of rudeness; I'm talking about rudeness born out of desperation![17]

When I was a pastor, I longed to see our church become a "praying church." I asked the Lord, "How is it that when well-known ministers come to town, our church is packed; but when we call a prayer meeting, it's 'me and my three'?" God seemed to reply with a question of His own: "Do you really want the church to pray?" When I said yes, He said, "Do you know why the church is not praying? It is because *they don't see you and the other pastors praying.*"

The very next Sunday I asked the congregation, "Who would like to pray?" Nearly everyone raised their hands, so I said, "Okay, I will make a deal with you. I will pray *with you* at any time you want to pray, whether it is during the day or at night."

I took my sleeping gear to the church the next week and began to pray day and night. It was amazing to see how many people showed up to pray. On one Monday night, 30 men prayed with me until one o'clock in the morning; then they all went to work that morning as usual! At other times, people would hear from God and come knocking on the church door at four in the morning. Although I was half asleep and not sure where I was, I would begin to pace around the prayer room and start praying up a storm. It was worth it because it released a spirit of prayer in our church. Long after we had been sent out from that church, an elder was appointed to pray with the people once a week around the clock. We need to allow God's zeal to consume us, no matter what the cost.

We need to have zeal for prayer, for the kingdom of God and for the lost. When *God's zeal begins to consume us, a spirit of servanthood will rise up within us.* I've noticed that every great servant of God in the Bible and in the modern Church exhibited a consuming zeal for God. As the zeal of God consumes us, may the Church and the hurting world around us see less of us and more of Him.

3. A servant never tries to be equal with the one he serves.

David held Saul's life in his hands on two separate occasions (recorded in 1 Samuel 24 and 26), yet David spared him because Saul was God's anointed and David felt he was to serve him as much as Saul would allow.

The first time David spared Saul's life occurred in the wilderness of Ziph when Saul entered a cave to relieve himself. He didn't know that David and his men were hiding in the recesses of the cave. David's men told him that God had delivered Saul, his enemy, into his hands and they urged him to kill Saul. David couldn't resist cutting off a piece of Saul's robe in secrecy to show him what he could have done to Saul if he had wanted.

Even that apparently harmless act brought conviction to David and he shared the essence of his servant heart with his men: "The LORD forbid that I should do this thing to my master, the LORD's anointed, to stretch out my hand against him, seeing he is the anointed of the LORD."[18] Then David held back his men and made them leave Saul alone. Saul left the cave still unaware of David's presence until David followed him out of the cave and cried, "My lord the king!"[19] Then David actually bowed down before the man who wanted to kill him; he put his face to the ground in humility and told Saul his life had been spared. *David refused to reach for equality with the one whom God sent him to serve* (even when it was seemingly within arm's reach)!

In the second incident, David walked right through 3,000 soldiers and into the center of King Saul's camp in the wilderness of En-gedi. The king's goal, once again, was to hunt down and kill David.

As David stood over the sleeping forms of King Saul and Abner, his general, one of David's mighty men named Abishai told him that God had delivered the king into his hands (again). Then he begged David to let him kill King Saul with his own spear. David again gave the response of a true servant to both God and man: "Do not destroy him; for who can stretch out his hand against the LORD's anointed, and be guiltless?"[20]

Despite the fact that the man sleeping at David's feet had hunted him like an animal for years, David still insisted on honoring King Saul as God's anointed. He knew that God would deal with Saul in His own time and in His own way. In the meantime, no man should harm the king.

The apostle Paul tells us to have the same attitude as Jesus, who chose to make Himself a bondservant to save others:

> Let this mind be in you which was also in Christ Jesus, who, being in the form of God, did not consider it robbery to be equal with God, but made Himself of no reputation, taking the form of a *bondservant*, and coming in the likeness of men. And being found in appearance as a man, He humbled Himself and became obedient to the point of death, even the death of the cross.[21]

A young "son in the Lord" to me serves as the senior pastor of a fine church in South Africa. One day he told me, "Dave, I can see that you are a 'father' in my life." I said, "What is all this 'father' business? Let's just be friends." He insisted, "No, God has shown me that you are a spiritual father in my life. I want you to father me."

I shrugged off his suggestion for some time with the phrase, "No, let's just be friends." Yet every time I ministered in his church, he told his congregation, "This man is my father. If I ever get out of line, call this man."

After several years, I finally understood what God was doing, and I took up the mantle this spiritual son had given me. I realized that spiritual fatherhood is given by a son; it is not imposed by a father. In the same way, "sonship" is always received and not imposed. David always considered Saul to be a father in his life, even though in later years Saul refused to live up to his calling.

Over the years I've noticed that my spiritual son has also become a spiritual father in his church, although many of his spiritual sons are older than he. Men respond to him and draw out the spiritual fatherhood he carries in his life. It happened because he was prepared to submit and become a son. He never tries to be equal with me, although he has certainly earned it in terms of his accomplishments and growth. David always recognized God's mantle on Saul. He was prepared to look beyond their earthly conflict and the issues of the flesh to honor God's anointing in Saul's life.

4. A servant cares.
When David sought refuge from Saul in the cave of Adullam, the Bible says his brothers and his entire family joined him along with "everyone who was in distress, everyone who was in debt, and everyone who was discontented."[22] Whether he liked it or not, David became the "captain" of nearly 400 men who are what I call the "can't works, the don't works and the won't works."

Somehow David managed to care for these men and their families, and he transformed them into one of the most feared and respected fighting forces in the land. David built lasting relationships with battered and bruised people whom others had judged and dismissed because of their creed, station, crimes or chronic failures. He loved the unwanted and they rose up to meet the challenge.

Three of the men in that cave became David's mighty men of renown: Adino, Eleazar and Shammah. These were the men who risked their lives to break through the Philistine lines simply to get David a drink from the waters of Bethlehem.[23]

He cared enough to teach them *self-worth* and *boldness* (along with the best training on prayer, worship and praise available), so they could meet life's challenges with courage and confidence. God used David's caring example to transform a defeated band of "losers" into the powerful army that helped him defeat all of Israel's enemies after he became king of Israel. As his three mighty men demonstrated by their selfless act of courage at Bethlehem, David also taught them not to count the cost of servanthood.[24]

A Vision of Jesus Crying over Kuwait

Carol and I felt we needed to reestablish our home base after spending several years on the road. We modified our schedule so that we could work from a central base and then we moved back into our home in South Africa, so our children could stay home. We decided to take two months off to strengthen our family and fix up our home, which was showing the effects of some serious neglect.

On our eighth night at home, God began to speak to me. Everything was still in boxes, and Carol had gone to bed early, when suddenly I saw a picture of Jesus crying over the Middle Eastern nation of Kuwait. I woke Carol and said, "I've seen a vision of Jesus crying over Kuwait." She just said, "Oh, go to sleep, Dave!"

Neither of us slept that night because we both sensed the Lord was asking us, "Whom shall I send?" The following morning we prayed, "Lord, here we are. We are available. Send us." Christmas day was only 10 days away, and we began to pray and fast for direction. Finally, at about four o'clock on New Year's morning, we both sensed the Lord say, "I want you to go now." (This was before the beginning of the Gulf War.)

We trusted God to supply the airfare, and it eventually arrived. In those days you could not travel very far on a South African passport, so I decided to fly to London and search for a way into the Middle East from there.

I looked into Carol's eyes at Johannesburg International Airport and said, "If you don't want me to go, I'll stay." She looked frightened, but I'll never forget what she said: "Dave, I know before God that you have to go. In the natural I don't *want* you to go, but I know that you *have* to go."

The Gulf War erupted just as I arrived in London, and I asked God, "What do I do now?" He said, "The circumstances may have changed, but I have not changed My mind. Keep going."

By divine appointment, I met a major-general in the British armed forces in London. He had commanded some of the British troops involved in the Falkland War. He made arrangements for me to reach Kurdistan on the Iraqi border, where much of the action took place. I didn't realize it, but God permitted me to walk right into the middle of an unreached people group where I was able to share the gospel of Jesus.

After the war, a man in London sent a letter to Carol and me, saying he knew of 20 people who received Christ because of my work in Kurdistan during the Gulf War. That opened the door for Operation Mobilization and YWAM (Youth With A Mission) to enter the formerly closed area and establish permanent ministry bases.

Sometimes we have to move in the servant love of Jesus even when we don't know why and have no way of counting the cost. Carol realized this when a dear friend came to her while I was in Kurdistan and said, "If David is *in God's will*, he is safer in that conflict than he would be right here if he was *out of God's will*. He could walk across that street and get hit by a car if he were out of God's will."

5. A servant blesses.

After David became king of Israel and peace prevailed in the land, he remembered his covenant with Saul's son Jonathan and he began to search for any of Saul's descendants who were still alive. It didn't matter that Saul had done everything in his power to kill and discredit him. He had a promise to keep. His counselors said that Saul had one grandson (the only son of Jonathan), Mephibosheth, who was still alive. He had been crippled at the age of five when his nurse dropped him on the day of Saul's death; he was living in virtual exile.

When Mephibosheth answered King David's summons, he probably wondered whether he would see another sunrise. He immediately prostrated himself before David, but the king told him not to fear and promised to restore to him all of the property of his grandfather, King Saul. Then David said to Mephibosheth that he would eat at his royal table "like one of the king's sons."[25]

Any follower of Christ with a true servant heart is quick to forgive and forget the wounds and wrongs inflicted by others. God's servants always *choose to bless*, whether that involves doing acts of kindness, bringing joy to others or actively loving the unlovable through tangible acts of service.

All of this is virtually impossible to teach; it must be caught. Draw near to the divine Servant who gave His all for you. Let His fire ignite the flame of humble servanthood in your heart; then find someone else and serve them as Jesus served you.

Notes
   1. See Luke 9:23.
   2. Matthew 5:41.
   3. See Matthew 11:29,30.
   4. John 2:17, quoting Psalm 69:9.

5. See 1 Corinthians 12:28. The apostle Paul included the "ministry of helps" in his list of supernatural ministries in the Church that are ordained and empowered by God.
6. Matthew 5:39.
7. See 1 Corinthians 6:20; 7:23.
8. Matthew 20:26-28, bold mine.
9. 1 Samuel 16:7, italics mine.
10. 1 Samuel 16:13, italics mine.
11. 1 Samuel 16:19, italics mine.
12. See 1 Samuel 16:21.
13. Twice Saul threw spears at David (see 1 Samuel 18:10-16, 19:9,10) and sent messengers or servants to kill him (1 Samuel 19:1-7,11-17). He also schemed to have David fight against the Philistines unaided (1 Samuel 18:17-30), went to Samuel's house to kill him (1 Samuel 19:18-24) and ordered Jonathan to bring David back to the palace so he could kill him there (1 Samuel 20:30,31).
14. See 1 Chronicles 13:2,3.
15. See 1 Chronicles 13:5-11.
16. 2 Samuel 6:14.
17. Tommy Tenney, *The God Chasers* (Shippensburg, PA: Destiny Image Publishers, Fresh Bread Publishing, 1998), p. 27.
18. 1 Samuel 24:6.
19. 1 Samuel 24:8.
20. 1 Samuel 26:9.
21. Philippians 2:5-8, italics mine.
22. 1 Samuel 22:2.
23. See 2 Samuel 23:15-17.
24. In Luke 14:28, the Lord Jesus commands us to "count the cost," which appears to contradict what I am saying in this chapter. Please understand that Jesus was talking about the total, all-out commitment He requires of us when we receive Him as Lord and Savior. Once we make that decision, He expects us to obey and follow Him by *faith*, not stopping to count the cost or figure out our own way of doing things before we obey. If you are studying the biblical aspects of servanthood, I am assuming that you have already counted the cost and have given your all to Christ.
25. 2 Samuel 9:11.

CHAPTER FOUR

SERVING WITH DIGNITY AND DELIGHT

One of the problems with the Church today is that anyone who hopes to have a genuine encounter with Jesus Christ has first to wade through the muck and mire of who and what we are. Since we almost always act like lords instead of servants, by the time these people actually meet Jesus, many of them share the opinion of the late Indian nationalist leader Mahatma Gandhi, who said, "I like Christianity; I would be a Christian if it were not for Christians."

The attitude of a servant determines the atmosphere of the palace. If you have the opportunity to visit the residence of a king, a president, a prime minister or a wealthy business leader, your first impression of that person will not be affected so much by the beauty of the palace or residence as by the attitude of the lowest servant.

Who is the first person you see when you walk into such places? It certainly isn't the master of the house. Most likely the first face you see (indeed the second, third and possibly the fourth face you see) will belong to a *servant*. When you finally see the noted leader or financier, your first impressions will have already been formed, solidified, cemented and sealed by the attitudes of the servants you have already met.

The same is true for people who come to our churches hoping to meet the gentle Master of the house. The crucial difference hinges on whether we serve our Master grudgingly or with dignity and delight.

One time I took a small group of people to a restaurant about 20 minutes before closing. It was obvious that we were unwelcome because our arrival interfered with their plans to leave promptly that night. I thought to myself, *If I were the owner of this restaurant, there would be several people who would no longer work here. They are only interested in their own enterprises, not in serving the needs of the customers.*

Do You Know Who Pays Your Salary?

The belligerent waitress who finally waited on us had such a sour demeanor that I decided to talk to her about it. "Ma'am, I know you're frustrated, but we're hungry," I said. "We came in here to eat, and you are still open."

"Technically, yes, we are still open," she said.

Her answer not only alienated me, but it also inspired me. Then I asked her a simple question: "Do you know who pays your salary?"

"Yes, the boss, the owner."

"No, he doesn't pay you," I said. "The customers pay you. The money he gives you comes directly from us. You think you're *serving him* and therefore you're ready to go home. Really, you should be thinking of *serving us*."

Our church pews are filled with Christians who say they are "serving the Boss," but they don't give a second thought for the lost. They don't understand the concept that the "customer" who walks in the door of God's "bread store," hungry, broken and needing help, is *the purpose* behind it all!

We mouth our praises to the Boss; we bow in obeisance and collect our "blessing paycheck" week after week while we turn away customers because they disrupt our plans for a timely departure from the store. If God were an earthly boss, He would wonder why His business wasn't prospering and growing. After all, He paid a handsome price to plant it on this bloody piece of real estate.

DIGNITY IN SERVANTHOOD CAN BE HARD TO COME BY

You and I determine the atmosphere of God's house by the way we serve others. How is your serve? Do you do it grudgingly or with dignity and delight? Dignity can be hard to come by when you accept the full terms of godly servanthood.

Servants in biblical times often had little or no clothing. According to some of the historical reference books I've read, it wasn't uncommon for servants of that era to go about their duties unclothed! It isn't easy to practice dignity while living in humility.

Have you experienced the joy of going to a hospital for medical tests and waiting in the corridor while wearing one of those too-small gowns that is trying to cover too much? It's difficult to describe any other experience that so suddenly and effectively puts everyone on equal ground.

I remember the time I underwent some tests for my annual physical examination. Sure enough, I found myself uneasily wearing the latest in hospital-gown fashions and sitting next to another man who was equally uncomfortable in his open-backed hospital gown. We were both forced to leave back in the dressing rooms our positions in life. I had lost my dignity as a preacher, and he had been stripped of his dignity as one of the leading politicians of an island nation in the Caribbean.

Under any other circumstances, I don't think he would have given me the time of day. We lived in two different worlds. On that particular day, however, our worlds collided in the indignity of a "no modesty" waiting room, and we suddenly became friends. In fact, we remained friends after we reclaimed our clothing and a measure of our dignity. My new friend has even entrusted me with certain aspects of his business in the States at times when he couldn't make it here.

It is difficult, but it's not impossible, to practice dignity while living in humility. Those who endure the indignity of humility together often enjoy a high level of camaraderie. If we can realize that in Christ we are *all servants*, the development of lasting relationships will get easier.

Our Savior Died in a State of Nakedness, Yet He Died in Divine Dignity

This is the catalytic balance, the dynamic of the Cross: to die with dignity while living in humility. I remember one writer wrote about "the naked splendor of the cross." Most artists today modestly paint a loincloth over Jesus' body on the cross. My understanding from Scripture is that He died totally naked within sight of everyone who passed by, yet He died in divine dignity.

It is not enough just to die to the flesh; we must die with dignity. Servanthood forces us to continuously die to our flesh, to our pride and to our own wishes and agendas. It is the cross of Christ delivered to our door—the court summons served on a daily basis. If we become servants at all, we tend to do it while hiding behind the cloak of arrogance: *I have to do this or the Boss won't like it.*

Sometimes the nakedness or transparency that servanthood requires can be embarrassing. I just read the early drafts of a book being written by a well-known Christian family, and I remarked to them that I was amazed by the transparency they were displaying in this book.

We live and serve others in the same way we stand in front of a photographer's camera for a portrait. We may be fully clothed, but we still suck in our bellies, puff out our chests and raise up our chins in hopes of putting our best foot forward. Most of us don't have a physique sculpted by Michelangelo. Our bodies tend to go in where we should be out, and we are definitely out where we should be in.

If you intend to obey God's call to servanthood, then at some point you must stop trying to hide your deformities and simply become who you are. We are called to say "I'm just a servant; can I help?"

LOVE MAKES THE MENIAL MAGNIFICENT

When we do this properly, we make the menial magnificent! Picture with me the gentle hand of a caretaker, smoothing the brow of his beloved spouse during their last days together. Although she is bedridden and unable to respond and will never again reciprocate with loving glances or gentle touches, her spouse's gentle service to her dignifies her in the midst of her pain. Countless times I have observed incredible dignity at the edge of a deathbed. Even the sight of a caretaker's loving hand wiping a face with a cool cloth—a seemingly menial task—is transformed into a magnificent act that brings tears to my eyes.

Jesus, the Master of our house, has literally entrusted His reputation to us as His servants.[1] We must learn to traffic in the joy of serving others with dignity and delight, so we won't become a stumbling block to those who seek Him.

DAVID SPEAKS

During a trip to London, my son, Ron, and I received a surprise lesson in the beauty of dignity from an unexpected source. To our delight, we saw the Grenadier guards come marching toward us with their fabled bright red tunics and tall black hats.

That was enough to thrill us, but then their band began to play "Happy Birthday"! To our surprise, the Queen Mother suddenly appeared.[2] It was her birthday, and this dear old mother of the nation who was well into her nineties celebrated her birthday by mingling with the crowd on London's streets. As I watched her, I was deeply struck by the *dignity* with which she carried herself—even in the midst of a crowd.

Jesus Served with Dignity and Delight

Dignity is something we expect of royalty, but we rarely associate it with servants. Jesus was a king, but He was also a servant who served with dignity and delight. I was reminded of this when I stopped in Texas on my way back from Haiti after the invasion of Haiti by United Nations and United States forces.

I met my friend Max Greiner and had the privilege of viewing his beautiful sculpture "Divine Servant." His life-sized bronze of Jesus washing Peter's feet has won acclaim around the world. As I studied the bronze and considered the man of faith who created it, I realized that Max's sculpture was not simply an art piece. After I returned to South Africa, I told Carol, "It is far more than art. It is a prophetic statement—like what we do with the cross and bowl." (I said this partly because I noticed that when Max began to pray for people near this art piece, miracles began to take place.)

Servanthood should not be something that we do; it should be something that we are.

Several weeks later, the Lord challenged me with the words "Over the years, you have seen many thousands of people come to know Me. You have seen whole cities come to revival, but *where are all the servants?*" I began to wrestle with this question in prayer and finally I sensed the Lord make a promise: "If you are faithful to do what I am about to show you, then you *will see a harvest of thousands of servants.*"

These words prompted me to pray and fast for 12 days, and the Lord began to birth in me the concept that servanthood is a celebration. He told me, "Now go and show the people that it's a *delight.*"

Many people don't serve in their churches or on the street because their concept of those who serve is that of a dull, boring, sour-faced little old lady with her hair tightly pinned in a gray bun on her head. The stereotype isn't true and it isn't fair either—I know a lot of very motivated and gifted little old ladies who wear their hair in a bun.

GODLY SERVICE IS A DIVINE DELIGHT

When I continued to wait on the Lord, He led me to reflect on the great servants of the Bible. None of them considered service to God or to others to be a drudgery; it was a divine delight for them to serve:

- Ruth *delighted* to serve Naomi.
- Jesus *delighted* to serve His disciples.
- Joseph *delighted* to serve Pharaoh.
- Elisha *delighted* to serve Elijah.
- Timothy *delighted* to serve Paul.
- David *delighted* to serve the things of his God.

They all considered it an honor to serve because **servanthood rightly done is not a drudgery, it is a dignity and a delight.**

The Lord also revealed to me that servanthood *should not be something that we do; it should be something that we are.* That happens when we commit ourselves to God's principles of sacrificial service and allow Him to change our "spiritual DNA," transforming us into anointed servants of God.

The life of Joseph provides one of the most complete pictures of godly servanthood in the Bible. You may think of Joseph as the little boy with a multicolored coat who was thrown in a well or as an interpreter of great dreams or as a great ruler. *Joseph was all of these things; but his greatest accomplishments came when he was a servant.*

Joseph served in two major areas: a personal servant to others and a servant to his own family. His family-serving ministry got off to a rocky start after he dreamed as a little boy that his older brothers would one day bow down to him. He unwisely shared the revelation with his brothers and ended up in the bottom of a well and was then sold into slavery.

A SON BY BIRTH, A SERVANT BY REBIRTH

Joseph didn't understand in his youth what he clearly understood in his maturity. As Tommy and I talked about this, Tommy explained it this way:

> You really can't go from being a son to being a sovereign. You must go from being a son to being a servant, and from being a servant to being *a sovereign who is a son by birth but a servant by rebirth.* Joseph didn't go straight to the regent's throne over Egypt; he went to the top through the servant's entrance. Centuries later, Jesus left His throne in heaven, passed through the servant's entrance and took up His serving towel before offering His life for us on the cross. Only then did He ascend to His throne at the right hand of the Father once again.

Joseph graduated from his desert pit to the position of a slave. Yet the Bible says he found favor and was promoted to *personal servant* for the king of Egypt's captain of the guard, Potiphar: "So Joseph found favor in his sight, and *served him.* Then he made him *overseer* of his house, and all that he had he put under his authority. So it was, from the time that he had made him overseer of his house and all that he had, that *the LORD blessed the Egyptian's house for Joseph's sake.*"[3]

Joseph had a true servant heart, and God prospered everything Joseph touched. Yet even godly people run into tests and trials at times. When Potiphar's wife tried to impose herself on Joseph, he resisted her advances. When she falsely accused him of assault, Joseph found himself locked up in prison unjustly. Yet his *serving* continued.

A Servant Heart Always Comes Through

God gave Joseph favor with the keeper of the prison, who *put Joseph in charge of everything in the prison* and didn't even bother to check up on him.[4] Then the king's chief butler and cook offended their master and landed in the king's prison with Joseph. The Bible says, "And the captain of the guard charged Joseph with them, *and he served them;* so they were in custody for a while."[5] (Tommy asked me, "How bad must a cook's cooking be to earn him a jail sentence?")

Joseph's servant heart came through time after time, whether he was serving in a private home or a prison cell. God gave him keen insight into the dreams of the butler and the cook, and both of his interpretations came to pass. The bad cook was hanged and the butler was restored to his former place of honor. Two years passed before the butler remembered Joseph and mentioned him to the king, who was being troubled by bad dreams. Joseph accurately interpreted the king's dreams and was appointed prime minister—at the age of 30—over all of Egypt.[6]

Joseph wisely set aside food reserves in every city of Egypt during the seven years of plenty revealed by God in Pharaoh's dream. Seven years of severe famine followed, which was also revealed by Joseph's interpretation of Pharaoh's dream. Joseph conducted himself as a *faithful servant* in all of his duties, even though he held greater power than anyone in Egypt except for Pharaoh himself, and God blessed everything he did. When the famine struck Joseph's family, they heard about the abundance of food in Egypt. Jacob, Joseph's father, sent 10 of Joseph's 11 brothers there on a mission to buy food.[7]

When Joseph's brothers were ushered in to his presence, they did not recognize him, for they assumed he was dead. He did not reveal his identity but, instead, accused his brothers of being spies. Joseph finally agreed to provide Jacob's sons with grain but required them to return home and bring their youngest brother to him. Then he took Simeon, the second born of the brothers, and held him in Egypt to guarantee their return.[8]

After a series of amazing tests, the brothers returned to Egypt in great fear with their youngest brother, Benjamin. Joseph arranged to meet with them at his own home and had a meal prepared in advance for their arrival. What happens next defines how the true heart of a servant acts regardless of status or circumstances.

Joseph Served His Family

After a dramatic reunion, when Joseph revealed his identity to his brothers, he told them:

> But God sent me ahead of you *to preserve for you a remnant on earth and to save your lives by a great deliverance.* So then, it was not you who sent me here, but God. He made me father to Pharaoh, lord of his entire household and ruler of all Egypt. Now hurry back to my father and say to him, "This is what your son Joseph says: God has made me lord of all Egypt. Come down to me; don't delay. You shall live in the region of Goshen and be near me—you, your children and grandchildren, your flocks and herds, and all you have."[9]

Joseph faithfully **served the world** when he was in Potiphar's house, in Pharaoh's prison and in Pharaoh's palace. In the end, he also **served his family** with the same godly faithfulness. Are we doing the same or are we mostly serving ourselves? I've noticed there are four biblical characteristics of a true servant that are easily seen by saint and sinner alike. We should do a self-check of our lives to see whether or not we measure up to God's standards of servanthood. I call these characteristics "Four Ways to Recognize a Servant."

1. A servant serves with joy.

The book of Isaiah says, "Behold, My servants shall *sing for joy* of heart."[10] Any servant who recognizes the One he serves will be joyful. Jesus said we should do everything as if we were doing it for Him.[11] As true servants, we should always serve with a spontaneous joy so that our service of love continues to be *a dignity and a delight.*

I have a pastor friend in Durban, South Africa, who went away on an extended trip with his wife for about six weeks. When he returned, he was looking forward to receiving a warm reception from his family and the church elders at the airport. They cleared customs and picked up their baggage, but no one seemed to be waiting for them.

Then my friend noticed a man in a top hat, white gloves and a formal tuxedo. He was holding a small sign *with my friend's name written on it!* My friend wondered if there was some mistake, but in the end he decided to introduce himself. The man promptly thanked him and picked up their bags and led them to a Rolls Royce limousine parked just outside the airport. The pastor and his wife took their seats in the back and the Rolls headed toward their home.

By this time my friends were laughing like two teenagers on their way to the prom. When the Rolls Royce arrived at their home, they noticed a beautiful red carpet leading from the limousine to their front door. When they entered the house, the entire church leadership was waiting to surprise them.

Tables had been beautifully decked with marvelous cakes and the finest china. After an unforgettable homecoming celebration and only 20 minutes of fellowship, the elders announced that it was time to leave. The church leaders quickly cleaned up the house and kitchen and promptly left as promised—leaving behind them two thoroughly refreshed leaders who thanked God for the servants in their church. Spontaneous and joyful servants bring refreshment and new strength to those they serve.

The joy of servanthood took another form in a little village in Natal, South Africa. I visited a local church with a beautiful 500-seat auditorium, which was fairly large for the size of the town. The brick construction was so striking that I mentioned it to members of the congregation. To my surprise, they told me they built it themselves. That usually means a congregation hires an architect and works with him to draw up the plans and then raises the finances and hires a construction company to build it. When I asked about it, they said, "No, we built it with our own hands."

Most veterans of church building committees will tell you such projects nearly always generate an abundance of contention. When I asked my hosts how their congregation built the church building, they said they met every Saturday to work on the project. Some of the men mixed concrete, some pushed wheelbarrows, and others laid bricks. The ladies brought picnic baskets of food and fellowshiped while the children played.

When they told me this went on every Saturday for two years, I assumed that it must have been a fairly turbulent time in their history and said, "I imagine you were glad when it was all over." Their reply wasn't what I expected. "No, on the contrary, we were sorry when it was finished. *We loved the fellowship.*"

It was a *joy* for those church members to serve the Lord and one another every Saturday for 104 weeks, because it was *a dignity and a delight*. They were truly servants who served with joy.

2. A servant never asks, "What's in it for me?"

Joseph the servant chose to bless even during the time he was in his lowest place in the land and when God raised him up to the highest place in Egypt under Pharaoh. He never asked, "What's in it for me?" He simply chose to take on the mantle of a servant wherever he found himself, whether he was in a prison or Pharaoh's palace. God is interested in *servant leaders*. Jesus, the Son of God, became our ultimate example of selfless servant leadership in action.

Some years ago I had the privilege of carrying the cross and bowl from the Victoria Falls (Africa's equivalent to North America's Niagara Falls) to Lusaka. It would take about two-and-a-half months to cover the distance of several hundred miles. I needed an interpreter, and within a few days God sent me Vorster, a man of humble background and a stranger to me. He already had a job, but it didn't pay very much. (He later confided that he and his wife ate meat only twice a month—one of those days they had chicken and on the other they had fish. They lived on maize and porridge the rest of the time.)

Vorster was so determined to serve me that he took *unpaid* leave to walk with me as my interpreter. He never once asked, "What's in it for me?" although we encountered hardships of many kinds during our 13-week journey.

Carol finally joined us near the end of the trip, and donations finally started to come in as people became aware of the mission. At the end, Carol and I took stock of our finances and agreed that we wanted to bless Vorster. He had never asked for anything, including pay of any kind, but we felt the Lord say, "Give Vorster everything you have; just keep enough money to buy the gas you need to get home."

We immediately took everything we had and gave it to Vorster in obedience to God's command. We learned later that the gift was the equivalent of nine months' salary for him! The Lord chose to bless His servant Vorster because Vorster had never asked, "What's in it for me?" To be honest, it delighted us more than it did Vorster. We felt like parents who were too excited to open their own gifts because of the thrill they felt being able to give to their delighted children.

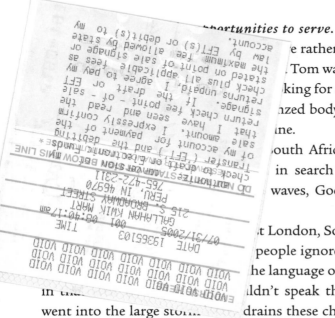

portunities to serve.

e rather than for opportunities

Tom was a young British surfer

king for a good surfing location.

azed body, he looked like he had

ne.

outh African coastal city of East

in search of "the perfect wave."

waves, God got hold of him and

t London, South Africa, he began to

people ignored. Most of them spoke

he language of the predominant tribe

in the ldn't speak the language at first, he

went into the large storm drains these children called home and befriended them. Most of "Tom's children" were also at risk because they sniffed the toxic fumes from petroleum-based glue and drank highly poisonous alcoholic drinks readily available on the streets.

Tom couldn't leave the children destitute, so he talked with officials of the national railway. They gave him some igloo-shaped structures which he bolted together to house the children. Then he acquired the help of a motherly lady to help care for the children.

He managed to raise enough money to build proper dormitory facilities and a facility to educate the children (most of whom had no schooling when he met them). He also recruited the help of some teachers to bring the children up to current standards, so they could enter the normal schools in the area.

Within a few years, Tom had cleaned up most of the streets and provided a godly living environment for most of East London's street children. Most of them received Jesus as their Savior in the process. Tom even spoke Xhosa as well as the locals by that time. He was just a young surfer who knew nothing about his call in the beginning, but he said yes to the Lord. Tom was a servant at heart *because he looked for opportunities to serve.*

God is more interested in the purity of our hearts than in our public performances.

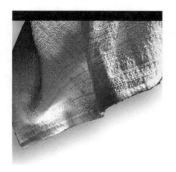

4. A servant serves when no one else is watching.

It is more important to walk with integrity in private than in public. Carol and I believe the things we do in our own home when no one else is watching are more important than the things we do for the whole world to see. The reason is simple: God is more interested in the purity of our hearts than in our public performances for people.

This reminds me of the senior associate pastor in our home church who also worked as my administrator for some years. The local congregation includes about 2,000 adults and is served by 13 full-time pastoral staff members.

One night we hosted a meeting with a prominent international guest. The meeting ran late, but afterward about 15 of us went to a local steakhouse for dinner. It was around midnight and we were having a great time. Then I noticed that our dear administrator friend, Keith, was not there. His wife was present, so I asked her where he was. She said, "Oh, he stayed at the church so that he could prepare the auditorium and straighten the seats for the next day's meeting." When I remarked that we had a janitor and other staff members in the church who could handle that, she said, "He just felt he wanted to do it."

Keith was working away at the church at midnight and no one else would have known about it had I not asked. He did it because he has a true servant heart. *It is what you do when no one else is looking that counts.*

When I go to England, I often stay with a dear friend named Gerry Armstrong. Early on I noticed that Gerry had a unique lifestyle. Every morning, he would rise early to make a cup of tea and some breakfast. When he was done, he would make another cup of tea and some breakfast portions and place it on a tray. Then he would carry the tray next door and serve breakfast to a little lady named Dorrie, who was in her 90s. While he was there, he always made sure everything in Dorrie's house was working and in good order before he went to work.

When he came home in the evening, he would make his wife a cup of tea and then set out another tray, which he again took to Dorrie. Before he left each evening, he carefully checked Dorrie's home once more to see that all was well within her house.

One day I said, "Gerry, apart from your salvation in Jesus, it will be the way that you serve this dear elderly lady when no one else is watching that will be remembered in heaven. You are being Jesus to her."

This principle—the importance of what you do when no one is looking—is especially true in the field of ministry. Very often we have enthusiastic young men offer their services to us for our next trip or mission after we minister as guests in church services around the world. Their zeal is noble, but very few of these young men are aware of the cost of discipleship.

We seldom share with church congregations the facts of the hardships and the pain we endure in the field because our primary goal is to encourage them. Therefore, few people realize that the ministry is mostly grit and not much glory. I remember the time I was traveling in a third-world nation with an interpreter who had an accident and soiled his bed one night. He was so embarrassed that he ran away because he felt he could not face me.

The Lord told me to wash his bed linens, even though they were in a disgusting condition. I obeyed the Lord and hung up the linens to dry. Then I made up the interpreter's bed with the fresh-smelling linen, and that evening he returned. The Lord told me to simply bless that precious man, and that love would cover for him. Most Christians who rarely minister outside of their churches don't see the other side of ministry. They don't see the times when people spit on you and swear at you. But *it's what you do when no one is looking that counts.*

"DO AS I DO"

On the day Jesus told the disciples that His hour had come, He did what no one in the room would have ever expected Him to do: He stripped off His outer garments and used a servant's towel to wash His disciple's feet. Afterward He said:

> If I then, your Lord and Teacher, have washed your feet, you also ought to wash one another's feet. For I have *given you an example,* that you should *do as I have done to you.*[12]

Jesus went on to tell them that *they would receive joy if they do these things.*[13] The word of the Lord is true. If we want to enjoy true joy within our lives, we need to take on the heart of a servant.

Have you noticed that everything seems to be "lite" these days? We have lite margarine, lite cola, lite beer and even certain candy bars are being marketed as lite. The problem is that to make something "lite," you must extract an essential ingredient and then introduce a substitute substance to create the impression that the product is the same. The pretense is that it tastes the same even though it doesn't have the right ingredients. The world loves to offer us something that allows us to indulge our senses, but the world fails to tell us the cost.

You simply cannot have Christianity without servanthood. Any so-called Christian gospel that fails to transform lives when it is preached is powerless. If you take into account the unmatched and unstoppable power of the Cross and the servant heart of Jesus, then any powerless gospel is by definition a "gospel lite." Someone has extracted so many nutrients that there is no heat or fire left. Others have removed the central ingredient while claiming their shortcut version is the same as the original. *There are no shortcuts to the foot of the Cross.*

Jesus knew His hour had come. He knew He had arrived at the point of His true destiny, and nothing was going to stop Him. Where are the people God is raising up who know their critical hour has come? Where are the God-chasing servants who pray in desperate passion, "I cannot live without Your presence, Lord! I cannot live without Your work in my life"?

We believe that God is going to begin to break through in mammoth proportions, far beyond anything previously experienced in the last century. Before that happens, however, God wants us to take up the cross of Christ and lay down the agenda of our flesh so that servanthood becomes *a dignity and a delight.* It is the only way our lives can make a difference.

I am not interested in "Christianity lite," and I have no desire to be a lightweight Christian. It is time for what God's Word calls "groanings which cannot be uttered."[14] That describes the divine desperation we experience in the Spirit when we begin to silently pray, *If You want to change anyone, **change me**, Father God. I don't care what it takes!*

Notes
1. See Romans 2:24.
2. The Queen Mother is the widow of the late King George VI, and the mother of Great Britain's reigning queen, Queen Elizabeth II.
3. Genesis 39:4,5, italics mine.

4. See Genesis 39:22,23.
5. Genesis 40:4, italics mine.
6. See Genesis 40:8—41:44.
7. See Genesis 41:46—42:3.
8. See Genesis 42:15-20.
9. Genesis 45:7-10, *NIV*, italics mine.
10. Isaiah 65:14, italics mine.
11. See Matthew 25:40.
12. John 13:14,15, italics mine.
13. See John 13:17.
14. Romans 8:26.

CHAPTER FIVE

SERVANTHOOD IS A HEART ATTITUDE, NOT AN APTITUDE

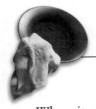

When it comes to flying an airplane, altitude adjustments are a fact of life for pilots of private and commercial aircraft. Those adjustments can make the difference between a safe flight and a fatal crash. Many times altitude adjustments come when pilots fly over new terrain, take a new course or prepare to end a flight. They may need to climb higher to avoid mountains or obstacles or fly lower in preparation for a landing.

There are also adjustments to be made on the way to becoming a servant. But these adjustments are of the *attitude* variety and are necessary to enable us to properly navigate our way through the changing terrain of the world around us. Change is a fact of life for us, but it requires that we have the insight or vision to perceive our need for an adjustment.

Compassion is the birthplace of miracles, and the heart is the womb of every miracle we will experience in this life. Before Jesus, as the Son of God, could raise Lazarus from the dead, He had to weep in grief as a son of man. *If a situation doesn't move you, then you can't move heaven.*

If you long to know "the problem you were born to solve," I can tell you that the key to your answer lies in the things that ignite your greatest passion. You see, conviction convinces you to *do something.* Conviction is a belief that is strong enough to die for and important enough to live for. It is often said, "You won't have a life worth living until you find a cause worth dying for."

Pharisees are historical proof that it is possible for religious people to say the right thing while doing the wrong thing.

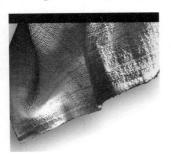

Christ died to be a servant; what higher calling can there be? We often want God to *preserve* us when what He wants to do is *prepare* us. Let me put it this way: If He spared not His own Son, *just who do you think you are?* Servanthood is our highest calling.

COMMITMENT, NOT DATING

Conviction convinces you to do something; and the logical outflow is commitment. Where God is concerned, commitment is not dating; it is *marriage*. God is not looking for a girlfriend; He wants a bride. Sadly, we have failed so miserably to love one another that our Lord says, "If someone says, 'I love God,' and hates his brother, he is a liar; for he who does not love his brother whom he has seen, how can he love God whom he has not seen?"[1]

The facade of the Pharisees was that they appeared to be religious and their words sounded right. The problem with the Pharisees was the hidden hand holding the dagger of judgmentalism behind the back of hypocritical religiosity. The Pharisees are historical proof that it is possible for religious people to say the right thing while doing the wrong thing.

Over the centuries, Pharisaic voices from the Church have thundered from its pulpits what the world "ought to be" while the Church's members and leaders often made no effort to meet those impossible standards themselves. Anytime we embrace the religious hypocrisy of the Pharisees, our reputation suffers. The irony is that if we followed the example of Christ and made of ourselves no reputation and became a servant,[2] then suddenly the reputation of the Church and everyone in it would be elevated to the heroic stature of the apostle Paul or Mother Teresa.

Servanthood is a heart attitude, not some occupational aptitude like flying a plane.

DAVID SPEAKS

It is difficult at best to do something when your heart just isn't in it. In a way, it is even worse when you have to work with someone whose heart isn't in the work. The Bible says, "For as [a man] thinks in his heart, so is he."[3]

My daughter, Carynne, went through this trial when she was a teenager. She was a lovely girl who was decent in every way, and Carol and I had done our best to raise her in the ways of the Lord. Carynne said the right things, prayed the right phrases and even did the right things. Even so, it was clear to us that our daughter was simply going through the motions. Her heart wasn't in it.

Finally, I told Carynne, "I want to release you from being a Christian. From now on, you don't have to go to church anymore. You don't have to do or say anything that is 'Christian' if you don't want to. I sense you are merely going through the motions, and these things are not life to you."

I explained that although she had been born again at the age of five or six, she needed to receive Jesus as an adult, now that she had become a young woman. She couldn't build her life on something that her mom and dad had wanted her to do as a little girl.

Carynne burst into tears in disbelief when she heard me say this, and I knew that I was taking a calculated risk. Nevertheless, I trusted her enough to let her rise to the challenge on her own.

In the weeks and months that followed, I noticed a dramatic change in my daughter's life. She received Jesus in an adult way, and she knew for herself that He was the redeemer of her sins and the loving Savior who died for her.

If my action seems somewhat judgmental to you, I can tell you it was probably one of the hardest things I have ever done. It isn't for everybody, but it was God's will for Carynne at the time. In the end, that "tough love" produced eternal fruit.

Servanthood is all about heart attitude. Unless your heart is changed, captured or broken by an encounter with God, then you will find it impossible to serve others according to God's will. Servanthood isn't about good works alone. Rotary Clubs and other civic organizations do an excellent job of doing good works, but their work is not biblical servanthood. True servanthood is an essential part of our discipleship under Christ. It is all about *allowing God to change our hearts.*

I've discovered at least four key components or essential ingredients that work together to form the heart attitude of a servant: compassion, conviction, commitment and love.

COMPASSION

Many of my adventures in God, with the cross and bowl, occurred after the Holy Spirit ignited compassion in my heart for a particular people or situation. It happened when I learned about the crisis facing the people in Montserrat, a tiny island nation near Antigua in the British West Indies.

A sudden volcanic explosion devastated the lives of approximately 12,000 people living on an island only 40 square miles in size. In a moment of time, an entire nation was put at risk of absolute displacement. So little of their lives remained that many of the residents were evacuated to distant places scattered across the world.

As the days went by, the compassion of the Holy Spirit in me for the devastated people of Montserrat grew stronger with every news report I saw. I couldn't shake it off or remove it—even for a moment. Finally I knew the Holy Spirit wanted me to take up the cross and bowl once again and make a prophetic statement of the servant love of Jesus to that tiny island nation.

I sensed that I was to share an ancient promise from God to Montserrat: "He sent His word and healed them, and delivered them from their destructions."[4] A second word of encouragement was given for me to share as well: "Who shall separate us from the love of Christ? Shall tribulation, or distress, or persecution, or famine, or nakedness, or peril, or sword?"[5]

We Immediately Felt Overwhelmed

A young man named Lee, who attended our home church in Port Elizabeth, South Africa, decided to accompany me on the mission to Montserrat. We quickly encountered the full onslaught of the enemy. Our best efforts to reach the island were delayed more than a week, but we managed to fly to Antigua and board a ferryboat to the island of Montserrat. As the ferry drew close, we could see mountainous billows of vapor still rising into the atmosphere from the volcano. We immediately felt overwhelmed.

The severe devastation on the island made it resemble the lifeless landscape of the moon. Everyone we met on the island had lost something precious. Compassion consumed us as we listened to endless stories of hopelessness and despair. Only the message of hope in Jesus would bring solace in this place.

I will never forget the sound of the howling wind or the hollow sound of a lone piece of sheet metal, what was left of a tin roof, banging in the breeze. Any remaining buildings in the worst areas of Plymouth, Montserrat's capital, were buried up to their windows in volcanic dust. The roof of one of the red pay-phone booths barely protruded from the surface of the dust in one location. Many of the debris-littered streets were deserted.

We felt overwhelmed by what we saw, but the pain we encountered in the people was far worse. Lee and I decided to visit one of the makeshift shelters at the northern end of the island. We talked with an elderly lady there who said the lava flow from the volcano literally buried her house and killed both of her sons. She had nothing; and when I asked what would happen to her, she said, "I guess life must go on."

One evening I hitched a ride with a man who had been the headmaster of Plymouth's technical college for 30 years. The volcano totally buried the college, and there were no plans or finances available to reconstruct it. That meant my new acquaintance was unemployed. He also told me that his son's feet were so severely burnt by the lava flow that he had to be evacuated to Canada for special treatment and plastic surgery.

As my compassion burned deeply within me, my resolve to serve these people kept growing stronger and stronger. My heart had changed. I felt overwhelmed, but I had no choice about the matter. *You cannot touch lives like this and not feel compassion.*

CONVICTION

The power of conviction shows up in virtually everything we do in the kingdom of God, but it is especially important when serving. I often counsel people, "Make absolutely sure that God told you to do this, because the day will come when you must hang on by the finest thread. The only thing that will keep you going is the fact that God told you to do it." *Only God-ordained conviction can help you persevere in your servant's call when everyone else has deserted you.*

I'm glad that Jesus is more interested in how we finish than in how we begin a thing. The level of our conviction can determine the success of our service in His name. We must be fully convicted about the things we feel God calls us to do. The harsh reality of this truth became clear during a difficult ministry walk through the African nation of Zambia. Once again, Vorster served as my interpreter; and a Scandinavian friend accompanied me on the trip.

Life became very difficult after we had walked for more than a month in blistering heat. Each tiny village we encountered seemed to be poorer and more devastated than the one before. Water and food were scarce, and even simple things like a Coca-Cola (which is generally available in Africa) were difficult to purchase at times.

As the pressures of the trip mounted, the sheer challenge of the distance we had to travel began to wear on Vorster. He felt so overwhelmed by the enormity of the situation that he felt he couldn't continue. Meanwhile, my Scandinavian friend, who was a marathon runner, began to feel the pressure of the unknown we faced every night. We simply didn't know where or if we would be able to sleep from day to day.

Neither of these men could be considered soft in any way. Both were mature men of God who had proven their faith and strength in previous service to the Lord. They were intensely loyal to the Lord and to me, but they couldn't decide whether to continue or quit. One weekend I decided to send my faithful interpreter back home. If I didn't do it, I knew he would stay through sheer loyalty to me, even to his own hurt. I gave him enough money to purchase his bus fare and provide food for his family; the intention of my heart was to bless him.

I Must Continue Because God Told Me to Do This

Then I suggested to my Scandinavian friend that we seek the heart of God for direction concerning his role in the trip. Every time I looked at him he would burst into tears and he just didn't know what to do. Before Vorster left on the bus, I told both of my companions that I loved them. Then I said, "I am determined to complete the course and mission, whether or not you continue, because God told me to do this." (I knew that I could not succeed without their help. I was voicing my *convictions* instead of my *circumstances*.)

When my Scandinavian friend and I began to pray on the morning after Vorster left, I clearly felt the Lord say to me, "Send him home." I loved my friend dearly and I knew that he loved me; but as I shared this with him, he continued to weep and I could see the relief on his face.

It took a giant step of faith for me to raise the money to purchase an international airplane ticket for my friend to return home—especially from the interior of Zambia. The following day I placed an urgent telephone call to my dear wife, Carol, and said, "I need your help." She asked about the safety of the situation and I told her I would rate it at 50-50. Her immediate response was, "I'll be there as soon as I can."

Within a matter of days my friend was headed home to Scandinavia and Carol had joined me. Meanwhile, Vorster sought the Lord's face when he reached his home and became convicted and convinced that he had to rejoin me as my interpreter. Carol, Vorster and I eventually arrived in Lusaka, Zambia's capital, with much fanfare, including television and newspaper coverage and a warm personal welcome from a government minister. We even had the joy of leading one of the interviewers to the Lord!

Vorster subsequently returned as a pastor to Zimba, one of the small villages we walked through during our long trip. He is doing an excellent job for the Lord there.

Only the conviction that comes from the Holy Spirit will pull us through the challenges of servanthood with the correct heart attitude.

Only the conviction that comes from the Holy Spirit will pull us through the challenges of servanthood with the correct heart attitude.

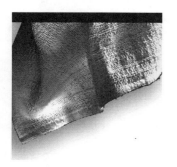

COMMITMENT

Commitment is a word that our generation treats like a dirty four-letter word. It wasn't always that way. It used to be that individuals would commit their careers to companies, and companies would reward that commitment with secure employment. I have an uncle who understood the meaning of commitment. He worked at one job from the age of 16 until his retirement at the age of 65. But stories like his have become increasingly rare. We live in a throwaway world. Employers throw away employees; employees choose any job that gives them a few dollars more. We dispose of cups, plates, knives and forks, napkins, diapers, jobs, friendships, pastors and even spouses.

People are afraid to make commitments to the Lord, to marriage, to job responsibilities and to parenting children. Once we commit our lives to Him, we often find it difficult to follow through, especially if it means we might face persecution or be required to serve others.

The Bible mentions a man of uncommon commitment named Ittai the Gittite. He and his band of 600 soldiers chose to stay with David even though the king was running for his life from his own son, Absalom. When David asked Ittai why he was staying with him and urged him to go home, Ittai said, "As the LORD lives, and as my lord the king lives, surely in whatever place my lord the king shall be, *whether in death or life, even there also your servant will be.*"[6]

During the Gulf War, I met a man who understood the commitment of servanthood on a level far beyond what most us will ever know. We met in the town of Adana in southern Turkey, near the northern borders of Syria and Iraq. The United States and Allied forces launched bombing raids into Baghdad from the military base of Ingelik near Adana.

What the Cross Means to Turkish Muslims

At that time, by our estimates, barely 300 people in Turkey followed Christ. In many ways, Turkey is the birthplace of Christianity in much the same way that the land of Israel is birthplace to Judaism. Yet today, Turkey is essentially a closed Muslim nation. Most Westerners do not realize that Turkish Muslims view people carrying crosses and sharing the good news of Jesus much as Jewish people view swastika-carrying members of neo-Nazi groups today. It was in Turkey that the crusaders came ashore with crosses on their helmets and shields and slaughtered hundreds of thousands of Turks in the name of Christianity. In others words, if you appear on Turkish streets carrying a cross and bowl, you become public enemy number one.

En route to Adana, I passed through Nicea, the namesake of the Christian Nicene Creed. Sadly, there was virtually no trace of Christianity left there. I found the same conspicuous absence of Christianity in Ephesus and in Antakya (Antioch), where Paul established the first church in what he called Asia (modern-day Turkey).

The ground war occurring in that region at the time paled in comparison to the centuries-old conflict in the heavenlies over Turkey. Satan had killed the Christians, stolen their faith and destroyed the work done by the Church fathers of earlier centuries.

After much prayer, I felt the Holy Spirit prompting me to carry the cross and bowl from Adana to Tarsus in southern Turkey, where the apostle Paul was born. "Lord," I said, "I can't go without an interpreter." Apart from my conversations with American soldiers stationed at the airbase, I had not heard English spoken for two weeks, nor had I found a single Christian in this city of almost a million people (not even a Catholic nun). I learned later that more Christian blood had been shed in this area than in any other part of Asia or the Middle East!

One morning I felt the Lord say, "Just take a stroll. Leave the cross and bowl behind and simply go for a walk."

I Realized He Was a Muslim

I stepped out into icy winter weather and began to stroll along the streets. To my surprise, someone behind me said, "How are you doing?" in English. When I turned around, I saw a young Turkish man who must have been about 21 years old. We resumed our walk and began talking. When he told me his name was Murat Ai, I figured he was a Muslim. The Holy Spirit "nudged" me and said, "This is your man"; and I silently protested, *He is a Muslim, Lord.* Yet once again, the Spirit said, "He is your man."

"Murat," I asked, "have you ever walked a long way?"

"Sure," he said. "I walk around Adana."

"No, I mean a *really long* way," I said.

"Where do you want to go?" he asked.

"Tarsus; and I need you to walk with me to interpret."

When Murat asked me why I didn't want to take the bus, I knew I couldn't tell him it was because the Lord told me to walk. I simply repeated that I just wanted to walk, and he asked how much I would pay him. We made a deal in American dollars, and I realized that I had to tell him the *whole* story before I could ask him to associate with a Christian missionary.

He Had Never Heard the Name of Jesus

"Murat," I said, "there is one thing you should know. I'm going to carry a wooden cross with a bowl."

"No problem," he said. "Business is business."

Still I pressed on: "Another thing I need to tell you is that I'm going to be telling the people about Jesus."

"What's that?" he asked. He had never heard the name of Jesus! I didn't go into too much detail at that point. I knew he would learn fast once we were out on the road.

When we began our long, cold and tedious journey a few days later, I felt the Lord tell me to carry the cross and bowl through the city in its unassembled state. He promised to show me where to assemble it. I followed those instructions, and when we reached a quiet alcove off the main street, I sensed I had found the place to assemble the cross and bowl.

I dropped to my knees to bolt it all together and then turned to see a circle of shoes and boots surrounding us. My heart started pounding and Murat wobbled nervously like a willow in the breeze. However, we quickly recovered from that anxious moment (and several similar ordeals that befell us during the trip).

Abducted and Stripped

One time we were abducted by a group of soldiers and stripped of everything we had—right down to our underwear. (We were able to retrieve
the most essential items later.)

The most significant event of the trip occurred in the back of a tiny
garage where we had settled down for the night. I turned to Murat and
said, "I want to tell you about Jesus." He sat patiently and listened for
three hours while I shared the amazing plan of salvation God had
designed for us through Jesus. I told him how Jesus came to Earth to set
us free and that He is the one true living God.

When I finished, I asked Murat what he thought. He simply said, "I
want to receive Jesus as my Lord and Savior."

"Before you do that," I said, "I want to point out a few things. Your
family will most likely disown you; your friends will reject you; you will
probably die for the commitment you are about to make."

"I know," Murat replied, "but from what I've seen and heard, *I know
it is true.*"

I heated some water on our little kerosene lamp and as he sat with
his feet in the bowl, he surrendered his heart to Jesus. Then I gave Murat
a small Bible I had smuggled into the country. It was written in his own
language. He read the Word at least three hours a day and constantly
asked questions. Never before had I seen such commitment and hunger
for the things of God.

Murat stayed with me for the full duration of the Gulf war, and he
even walked into Kurdistan with me. After he gave his heart to the Lord
and realized he was a Christian brother, he insisted on serving the Lord
alongside me without pay!

Would I Ever See My Family Again?

Every morning during the long weeks of the Gulf War, I read the words Paul
wrote to the Philippians and wiped away the tears that came to my eyes: "For
to me, to live is Christ, and to die is gain."[7] I read those words not knowing
if I would ever see Carol and my children again. It was the next verse that
kept me going: "But if I live on in the flesh, *this will mean fruit from my labor.*"[8]

I was simply not prepared to live in mediocrity, and neither was my new convert. We often rode the local buses during our trip and sat among passengers who wore their customary Islamic dress. They often asked Murat about the nature of my visit because I was so conspicuously different. He did his best to steer attention in another direction, but all the while we knew that someone could have plunged a knife into our backs at any time.

On the last night of the Gulf War, Murat decided to get off the bus and visit some relatives in one of the villages on the route. When we were half an hour away from the village, he said, "Dave, could I do two things with you before I leave the bus? I would like us to pray, and I would like us to read the Word of God together."

We bounced along on that Turkish bus in the darkness of night and read the Word of God using a little flashlight. Then we held hands and prayed, giving thanks to God for His sustaining mercy. I will never forget the young Turkish man named Murat who reflected the committed heart of a servant in the midst of danger.

LOVE

Have you heard the popular adage "People don't care how much you know until they know how much you care"? It is more than a nice saying; it is a *true saying*. Anyone who wants to serve is well advised to keep that statement fresh in his or her heart and mind.

The Bible says in essence that we can have compassion, conviction, commitment and every spiritual gift listed in the Book, every day of our lives; but *if we do not have love, we are nothing.*[9] Jesus put it this way: "Greater love has no one than this, than to lay down one's life for his friends."[10]

Earlier, I mentioned my friend Keith, who served as my ministry administrator at one time. His wife, Gill, is also an extraordinary servant who carries a unique mantle, or personal anointing, to minister to people in need.

On one particular evening, Gill was called out of a church service to counsel and minister to a 19-year-old woman who had been dumped on the church doorstep. She came from a dysfunctional family and it was obvious she had been abused. Her social skills were almost nonexistent and her value system was the reverse of what it should have been. Gill also learned that the girl knew virtually nothing about Jesus.

Laying Down Your Life for a Friend

Gill looked at the young girl as she clutched the tiny suitcase containing all of her earthly possessions. Gill had nowhere to send her, and the girl had nowhere to go. Finally, Gill decided to take her home for the night.

She didn't realize it, but she was about to lock herself and Keith into a three-month commitment with a young girl who required several hours of counseling and one-on-one mentoring every day. The girl eventually surrendered her heart to the Lord, and Gill painstakingly worked to lay new godly foundations for the young woman's value system.

They also bought her new clothes; and several months later, with the assistance of the church, they rented a small cottage for her. In addition, they managed to secure for her a job at a local pet shop.

More than two years after the process began, Gill and Keith still have lunch and extended fellowship with that young lady nearly every Sunday afternoon. Gill still looks out for her well-being, making sure that she has food on the table and that she is never left to be lonely during the holiday seasons of Easter, Christmas and New Year's. That young lady has grown in her faith and love for the Lord. Her countenance has changed and her self-esteem continues to grow to this day.

Where others would have faltered or given in to the temptation to write off such a "problem child" as too challenging or complicated, Gill and Keith chose to lay down their lives to help this young woman claim a new life in Christ. They could have chosen the easier road, but they chose the more difficult path of selfless servanthood. They understand what Jesus meant when He said, "Greater love has no one than this, than to lay down one's life for his friends."

The only way God can transform servanthood from something that we *do* to something that we *are* is if we will allow Him to *adjust the attitude of our hearts*.

Lord, we ask You to continually mold and reshape our hearts on Your potter's wheel. Once we emerge from Your skillful hands, may we too reflect the compassion, conviction, commitment and love of true servants after Your own heart.

Notes
1. 1 John 4:20.
2. See Philippians 2:7.
3. Proverbs 23:7.
4. Psalm 107:20.
5. Romans 8:35.
6. 2 Samuel 15:21, italics mine.
7. Philippians 1:21.
8. Philippians 1:22, italics mine.
9. See 1 Corinthians 13:1-3.
10. John 15:13.

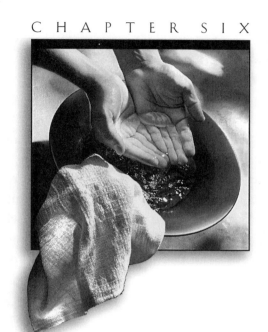

UNDERSTANDING
THE POWER OF SERVANTHOOD
AND THE IMPORTANCE
OF SHINING SHOES

ᴊ... ...s did some of His most important work while sitting at people's feet, sharing a meal. He didn't have a gilded office on the 77th floor in the Jerusalem business district; and as far as we know, He didn't have a desk, a secretary or even a home of His own. He tended to conduct a lot of family business around the dinner table.

One time His 12 disciples came in for dinner, and even though they remembered to leave their sandals outside, they brought in enough road dust and donkey and camel droppings on their feet to make the room especially fragrant.

Jesus must have noticed two more related problems: there seemed to be no servants available to do the foot-washing thing; and none of the disciples appeared to be ready to take the plunge of selflessness that night. That meant that Jesus was faced with the dual pollution problems of pride-stained hearts and filthy feet—on one of the most important nights of His ministry.

Somebody would have to do something to restore a proper atmosphere in that place. In the Lord's view, the solution was simple. He would clean up both messes at once through the power of servanthood:

[He] rose from supper and *laid aside His garments, took a towel and girded Himself.* After that, He poured water into a basin and began to *wash the disciples' feet,* and to *wipe them with the towel with which He was girded.*[1]

How Could the Son of God Stoop So Low?

Peter, the one who recognized the deity of Jesus before anyone else in the group, just couldn't understand how the Son of God could stoop so low as to wash donkey dung off the feet of His own disciples. Peter wasn't an expert in the area of the Law, but his logic screamed out, "Something's wrong with this picture!" Where are the servants when you need them? The other disciples could sit there and let this happen—but not Peter!

The disciple with the biggest mouth decided to gently put Jesus back in His place once again. (The first time, Peter tried to steer Jesus away from the "dying on the cross" idea and was rebuked.[2]) He asked Jesus if He really meant to wash his feet, in hopes that the Lord would take the hint. When Jesus said something about understanding later, Peter took the direct route he was best known for:

> Peter said to Him, "You shall never wash my feet!" Jesus answered him, "If I do not wash you, you have no part with Me."[3]

Jesus seemed to be very serious about foot washing, but I have to confess that I used to be like Peter where foot washing is concerned. Then God used my shoe-shine box to teach me an unforgettable lesson in servanthood.

Several years ago, when I was the pastor of a church, I had to make a decision that hurt the feelings of a man in my congregation. This man was honest and he meant well; but in this situation, his actions were wrong. After I made the needed course adjustment, my relationship with this man remained strained and difficult. I did what I knew to do to restore peace between us, but nothing seemed to work. Finally, I took it to the Lord.

HE SAID, "BE A SERVANT"

The Lord told me exactly what I did *not* want to hear; He said, "Be a servant." I did my best to become a servant, but nothing I did seemed to bring this man around. That is when the Lord stepped in and reminded me about the importance of shining shoes.

Travel is a necessary part of my ministry, so I have to spend a lot of time in airports. Occasionally I have my shoes shined by the people who operate shoe-shine booths in major airports, and I decided to ask one of them how much they made. I wasn't surprised when he just smiled, but I decided to come up with an estimate on my own.

If the man handled six customers an hour at $5 each, he is a $30-an-hour man. If he works five days a week and takes a two-week vacation every year, then he and his shoe box generate $60,000 in revenue per year before expenses and Uncle Sam!

When I mentioned my discovery to some of the teenagers in the church and suggested shoe shining as a way to generate some serious summer money, one of them expressed the same sentiment most Christians have toward servanthood. He said, "I am not shining shoes!" Then the Lord nudged me and said, *Would you, Tommy?*

I shared what happened next in my book *God's Dream Team: A Call to Unity*:

Then God reminded me about the man whose feelings I had hurt earlier. The Lord said, "Then shine *his* shoes." It took some doing.

The next Sunday, I came to church and brought my shoe-shine kit. In the process of preaching, I called that gentlemen up in front of the whole congregation and asked him to sit there while I preached. My message was on foot washing; my text from John 13. I "contemporized" foot washing to shoe shining. While I preached, I shined his shoes. I took off my coat, tucked in my tie and shined his shoes while I preached. He and I both knew what was going on even though the congregation at large did not.

As I shined his shoes, I began to weep; he began to weep. The Holy Spirit moved as the spirit of a servant was exemplified. The spirit of antagonism was broken. People began to line up to shine each other's shoes. They pulled out handkerchiefs to wipe off each other's shoes. Hot tears trickled onto dirty shoes. A spirit of unity came over our church. Great revival ensued.

How long has it been since you put up your sword and picked up a towel? His Kingdom is built with servants. Begin to wipe the debris from your brother's feet. If He did it, we should do it! Practice servanthood. Remember the symbol of His kingdom is a towel.[4]

THE CROSS IS THE SYMBOL OF OUR "FAMILY BUSINESS"

The Cross is the symbol of our translation, or deliverance, from darkness into light through Jesus' selfless sacrifice on Calvary. The towel is the symbol of our ongoing "family business" and individual occupation. As usual, God's way of doing things is totally different from the way we would do things.

I want to share something written by Gordon MacDonald that makes a lot of sense:

> [Jesus'] followers grew up in a culture that understood only one politic: power. The power of kings and armies—brute force. The power of the religious community—pronouncing or denying God's approval. The power of family, village, and tribal tradition—nailing people to mindless conformity to "the way we do things."[5]

Most of us still find it easier to relate to the sword than to the towel. We find it easier to point fiery fingers of righteous indignation at sinners and saints than to wash their feet, bind our brothers' wounds, feed hungry stomachs or clothe naked bodies.

Servant love requires us to strip off our hard-won religious robes and replace them with the garments of humility, naked vulnerability and servitude.

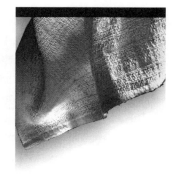

SERVANT LOVE GETS MESSY

For some reason, we find it easier to preach in order to prod people into the Kingdom than to love them into God's presence. Perhaps that is because servant love gets messy. It requires us to strip off our hard-won religious robes and replace them with the garments of humility, naked vulnerability and servitude. MacDonald put it this way:

Jesus' brand of servanthood means that everyone (child, leper, Gentile, opposite gender, sinner) is more important than me. Servanthood means that all I have and all I am is placed at your disposal if it will bring you into the presence of God. Servanthood is not about how I can add value to my life, but about how I add value to yours.[6]

| D A V I D   S P E A K S |

Tommy is absolutely right when he says that servant love can get messy. Once we finally agree to lay down our pride and pick up a servant's towel, we find that even in the serving we can be hard-pressed to deal with unwelcome changes, irritations and complications.

WE DISCOVER THE TRUTH UNDER THE PRESSURE OF THE UNEXPECTED

The Lord often allows us to step into situations where we must take stock of ourselves and check our heart motives. It is here, under the pressure of the unexpected, that we discover whether servanthood is merely what we do or it is what we really are. It is also in those moments that we learn where we truly place our trust.

This happened to me when I tried to transport my equipment to the volcano-ravaged island of Montserrat for the ministry trip I mentioned earlier. I like to have everything arrive together at foreign destinations, so I can launch my ministry trips with some degree of organization and preparation.

The first thing I do before I begin ministering is assemble my cross and bowl, strap on my water tanks and towels, and pack a good supply of Bibles (in the local language). Then I generally walk along a predetermined route provided in advance by the Lord. My ministry trip to Montserrat presented a totally different situation.

To reach Montserrat in the West Indies, we had to fly from South

Africa to New York City, and from New York to the island of Antigua. From there we had to board a ferryboat to take us to Montserrat.

When we arrived in Antigua, my friend Lee and I discovered that the trunk containing my water tanks, cross and towels had been mislaid en route from Europe to New York. To put it briefly, the trunk was found three times and lost four times between three airlines! At least once during the trip, we spoke to someone who actually had the trunk in his possession; this person then relabeled the trunk and personally watched it go down the conveyor belt en route to us—but it was lost *again* between New York and Antigua.

Our representative in Antigua actually saw the tags from our trunk on the desk of one of the airline officials, and I personally found the entry in the customs logbook where it had been received and logged in. Nevertheless, the trunk was nowhere to be found.

One airline official asked why I was so obsessed with finding this trunk. He assured me they would reimburse me for the contents and asked what they were. I asked him if he went to church; and when he said, "Not very often," I asked him if he knew about Moses.

How Do You Place a Value on a Wooden Cross?

He said he did, so I told him it would be similar to Moses' losing his rod when he was leading the children of Israel through the wilderness. I believe that God places His mantle of anointing on things just as He did on Aaron's rod. How do you place a value on a cross and bowl combination that has washed the feet of thousands of people and has seen lepers healed, marriages restored and whole cities come to revival? I had ministered to prostitutes, peasants and presidents with that cross and bowl. It may have had a worldly value of only $50, but I know that at that time, I would have gladly laid out $1 million and more to have it back (assuming I had such money of course).

We received permission to search through three bond stores and a major customs warehouse but to no avail. After a week of utter frustration involving numerous trips to and from the airport, followed by patience-stretching delays and dead ends in our search (and constant bombardment in the spirit realm), we decided to head for Montserrat anyway.

My habit in all the years I'd ministered around the world was to pack the cross and bowl in my check-in luggage, along with the rest of the equipment and supplies. I did this whether I was flying to locations in South Africa or to international ministry sites.

This time, however, I decided to pack the foot-washing bowl in my personal carry-on luggage. That meant that I still had the bowl, even though the cross, the portable water tanks, the towels and the Bibles were still keeping company with one of three airlines.

I just didn't know how I could operate without the rest of the gear. I *knew* God had brought me this far, but what now? I also asked myself, *Is my trust in the cross and all the gear, or is my trust in the Lord?* I had to do some deep soul-searching.

Still feeling devastated by the loss of my road gear and cross, I finally arrived on Montserrat with Lee. I felt as if my frame of reference had been pulled out from under me. I was having difficulty coping with my own emotions until I was confronted by the plight of the hurting people of Montserrat.

PUT ON YOUR BOOTS—WE'RE GOING ON A PRAYER WALK

The first morning after we arrived, I asked Lee if he had brought his hiking boots. When he confirmed that he had, I told him to put them on; we were going to take a prayer walk to discern the spiritual atmosphere. We walked all that day on some of the steepest, hottest terrain I had ever encountered.

We spent the following day in prayer and fasting, and I eventually felt the Lord say, *"I want you to leave My footprint on this island."* In practical terms, I was convinced the Lord wanted us to pray over every island house that was still standing after the volcano erupted, whether the house was occupied or not. It seemed a bit silly on the face of it, but we were to discover what God can do when His servants are tackle apparently menial tasks in obedience and joy.

The following morning, just before we left our room, I glanced down at my lonely bowl lying in the corner with a hand towel beside it. I felt the unction of the Holy Spirit urging me to take it with me.

I clutched my foot-washing bowl by the rim as we headed toward the first house in our path. Its lone occupant was a Rastafarian,[7] complete with the trademark dreadlocks. After some colorful discussion, he finally surrendered his heart to Jesus while I washed his feet.

A few houses further on we met a lady who said she had heard we were on the island. She had been waiting for us, so we prayed with her too and washed her feet. This went on all day long. Some of the shops managed to open despite the devastation of the volcano; and when the shopkeepers invited us in, the Lord allowed us to minister to them and wash their feet right in their shops. The Lord's favor went with us!

SPREAD THE WORD
BY ALL MEANS

One day a man unexpectedly came to us and announced that he had made an appointment for us to be interviewed on Radio Montserrat. To be honest, I wondered if the effort was even worth it. I suspected the worst, and when we arrived at the radio station, my worst fears seemed to be confirmed.

We found ourselves in a dilapidated old house that was serving as a makeshift studio (the volcano wiped out the original). The studio consisted of a solitary microphone mounted on a tabletop stand. It reminded me of the single-microphone sound systems common to older school auditoriums and church buildings. It definitely was not professional, but the Lord was about to show me once more that His ways are not my ways.

The two interviewers seated at the table appeared to be the worst part of the deal. When Lee and I took our seats across from them, it didn't take long for us to gather by their attitudes that they definitely were not Christians. In fact, they were somewhat hostile toward us.

As the interview progressed, however, I sensed the Holy Spirit bringing them under conviction and their attitudes beginning to change. Throughout the interview, I couldn't help but wonder in the back of my mind, *Is anyone even listening to this program?*

We had no idea of what God had up His proverbial sleeve. We learned later that Radio Montserrat was the *only radio station on the island.* We also discovered that since the station aired regular updates about volcanic activity and rescue operations throughout the day, the entire nation stayed glued to their radios!

WELCOME THE DAY OF PENTECOST MONTSERRAT-STYLE

There was something else we didn't know. Evidently the interviewers liked the interview with us so much that *they broadcast it for three days in a row* to their captive audience. By then, everyone on the island knew who we were. We had become like pop celebrities almost overnight. People actually stopped their cars to shake our hands when they saw us walking along the road. Others came running out of their homes, crying, "What must we do to be saved?" We felt like we were reliving the day of Pentecost all over again, Monserrat-style.

One lady called us into her house and asked us to minister to her. While we were praying for her, a man who had a notorious reputation in the area came to her door unexpectedly. He immediately fell to the ground under the conviction of the Holy Ghost and began to repent of his sins! We had the joy of washing his feet at his point of conversion.

Once again, the Lord made a way where there was no way. We came to Montserrat with nothing but the clothes on our backs, a foot-washing bowl and a towel. Yet God used these things—in the hands of somewhat bewildered but obedient servants—to release the power of servanthood and pour out His Spirit on an entire island nation. We felt a bit like

Peter and John at the gate called Beautiful where Peter told the crippled beggar, "Silver and gold I do not have, *but what I do have I give you:* In the name of Jesus Christ."[8]

T O M M Y   S P E A K S

Dave's experiences in Montserrat should cause us to ask, "What do we have to give to those we meet each day?" Is it time for you to pull out your shoe-shine kit and shed tears over the shoes of one you've hurt? Has God called you to step into the pain and grief of others, armed only with love and servanthood? Lay down your sword and take up your towel. Put your trust in what He has given to you; then give it away by faith.

Notes

1. John 13:4,5, italics mine.
2. See Matthew 16:21-23.
3. John 13:8.
4. Tommy Tenney, *God's Dream Team: A Call to Unity* (Ventura, CA: Regal Books, 1999), p. 74.
5. Gordon MacDonald, "The Politics of Servanthood," source unknown. Gordon MacDonald served as president of InterVarsity Christian Fellowship and is a senior fellow with Trinity Forum, a leadership academy that helps leaders engage the key issues of their personal and public lives in the context of faith. Founded in 1991 as a nonprofit organization, it fosters strategic programs and publications that further its mission: to contribute to the transformation and renewal of society through the transformation and renewal of national leaders.
6. Ibid.
7. A Rastafarian is an adherent of a religious cult that originated among African Jamaicans. Among other things, Rastafarians believe in the ritualistic use of marijuana, forbid the cutting of hair, and honor the late emperor of Ethiopia, Haile Selassie, as a god.
8. Acts 3:6, italics mine.

CHAPTER SEVEN

SEEING WHAT JESUS SEES

Sometimes you have to *see* the towel to *pick up* the towel.

Just the other day I walked toward my daughter's room to conduct a fatherly inspection. When I asked, "Have you cleaned your room?" she answered me with her characteristic bright eyes and cheery smile, "Yes, Daddy."

When I walked into her room, I was surprised to find things in total disarray. My daughter's clothes were scattered across the bed and on the floor; and despite her sparkling eyes and wonderful smile, my little girl's room was nothing less than messy. I called to her and said, "Honey, just look at your room; it's a wreck!" She looked at the crime scene and smiled once again before she said, "It's *fine*, Dad. It's clean enough for me!"

The difference between our two views had nothing to do with the room. We were looking at the same room through two *different sets of eyes*.

If you have children, then you have probably noticed how easily you can see a task that needs attention or pick out the lone misplaced shoe in the far corner of a room when your child can't even see it. The same thing happens when a child misplaces something important, such as a class notebook, a pair of glasses or today's school assignment. The universal, one-size-fits-all statement common to kids is "I can't find it anywhere." Inevitably, the item is found right where it was carelessly dropped or forgotten. My grandmother's favorite reply in such cases—a phrase I can still hear echoing in the caverns of my memory—was a classic nugget of parental wisdom: "It was so close to you that if it had been a snake, it would have bitten you."

You Must Have a Paradigm-Changing Experience with Christ

Many of us haven't learned the value of servanthood because we don't have "servant eyes." We simply don't see the need for or the value of serving God by serving others. I've found that you must have an eye-opening experience that changes your paradigm, or framework, of thought before you can become a servant or understand the power of servant-hood.

That is one of the reasons the Lord of glory laid aside His reputation and entered our world: He came to give us an eye-opening experience that would shatter our earthbound and self-centered paradigms.[1]

Jesus modeled servanthood throughout His ministry on Earth. At the close of His life and earthly ministry, He picked up a servant's towel and said in essence, "You guys didn't get it when Mary washed My feet with her tears. I guess I'll have to help you change your paradigm even more. Foot washing is not just for the Marys; it is for everyone. You all need to 'wash and be washed.'"

You have to see the towel to pick up the towel! Immaturity generally doesn't see what maturity sees. Jesus told His disciples, "Lift up your eyes and look at the fields, for they are already white for harvest!"[2] The "field" isn't the problem—it's the laborers who can't even see what is right before them.

SERVANTHOOD IN ITS TRUEST FORM IS AN EYE TEST

Let me make this analogy: Picture yourself in the optometrist's office with the familiar eye chart before you. If all you notice is the big letter *E*, your optometrist would quickly inform you there are a lot of other letters on that chart that you should be seeing. The divine call to servanthood and the call to Christianity, in its truest form, is an *eye test*.

Don't be surprised if you discover that you need your vision corrected; most of us do. I call it "putting on the glasses of Jesus." All of a sudden you can see things *as He sees them.* You will find yourself weeping over the things He weeps over, and rejoicing in the things that cause Him to rejoice.

Jesus rejoiced at times when the disciples couldn't figure out what made Him so happy. At other times, He wept while the disciples wracked their brains trying to figure out what was so sad. Jesus wasn't crazy or overemotional; He just saw things differently.

Many times, we Christians lock ourselves away in our Christian cubbyholes, bolt the doors, close the windows, pull the curtains around us and refuse to go outside because we're afraid of what is out there. If you are *afraid* of what is there, then you can't *affect* what is there. If the Son of God had to leave His world to enter ours, it stands to reason that you and I must leave our world of the pews to affect the world on the news—the world outside of our church socials and in-house evangelistic campaigns.

Unfortunately, those who do walk into that world sometimes enter it with the thundering, condemning voices of judgmental Christians. That explains why the world and the media executives in New York and Hollywood view the Church as judgmental. This is the irony of it all: *If they saw more servants among us, they would see more Jesus in us.* If they saw more of Jesus, then they would change their ways.

If the Son of God had to leave His world to enter ours, it stands to reason that you and I must leave our world of the pews to affect the world on the news.

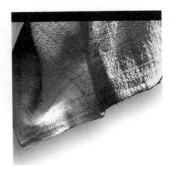

WE OVERLOOK WHAT WE DON'T WANT TO SEE

We tend to see the things we want to see, while totally overlooking the things we don't want to see. We like to read God's Word through our own personal filter. We read and catalog everything on the page that reinforces our own opinions. Meanwhile, our filter blocks out or skips over every verse that appears to contradict our preset assumptions, favorite doctrines and pet specialties.

These eye filters have a positive aspect to them at times. If you have an evangelistic anointing on your life, you probably search the Scriptures looking for "power" verses to help you invade the darkness with God's light. If you tend to be prophetic, you will look for straightforward black-and-white declarations to wayward believers and stubborn sinners. If you lean more toward the pastoral and nurturing area, you will look for verses on restoration, gentle healing and compassion. If you need a healing, it is obvious what filter you will be using during your study of the Word.

The problem is that when you look for what you already know is there, you become like the boy who buys a box of Cracker Jacks and dumps out the caramel corn and peanuts just to get the prize he knows is hidden inside.

Peter and John must have passed the gate Beautiful to enter Jerusalem's Temple of Herod thousands of times before the day *after* their encounter with the Holy Ghost in the Upper Room. On that special day, they saw the beggar who was crippled from birth and they saw something different. Before that time, he was the invisible irritation best soothed with alms and quickly forgotten lest he disturb the serene services scheduled inside the Temple.

PICK UP THE TOWEL OF SERVANTHOOD

The day after Pentecost, the two apostles must have said (in modern vernacular), "Oh man! We've passed this guy lots of times and didn't even see him." We know from the Scriptures that once their eyes were opened, Peter and John picked up the towel of servanthood and met the need they hadn't seen earlier.

Their obedience to *see* the need and *pick up the towel* of servanthood released a miraculous sequence of events that brought 5,000 more souls into the Kingdom and caused Peter and John to spend their first night in prison for preaching the gospel of Jesus Christ.[3]

Compassion is the motivating factor behind the miraculous, but the compassion of the heart is triggered by the perception of the eye. You have to be "moved" before you can react. Frankly, most of us are never moved because we move too fast. We blaze through life pursuing our own agendas while remaining blind and oblivious to what is going on around us.

We cruise past the world at 70 miles per hour and hurry our way on overpasses to avoid drug-infested poverty-ridden neighborhoods. It is quite different when you take the time to meet the real people who live in those places, and walk through their neighborhoods. Suddenly you *see* the hurting humanity in those "bad" neighborhoods. Be careful—your compassion possesses the power to shove your worst fears into a corner and propel you into the heart of the problem. Once there, compassion will demand that you help meet the needs of the people, in Jesus' name.

Jesus allowed His compassion to push aside His valid fears of what would happen to Him. He knew His greatest fear would come to pass if He kept going, but He continued toward the Cross anyway and was rejected and despised of men. It didn't matter. He came to Earth to be a servant and lay down His life "for the joy that was set before Him."[4]

Before we can be moved into a place of service, God allows us to see a need and become motivated by compassion. Unfortunately, when the world thinks of servants or service, they think of Rotarians who fund community projects or Shriners who build and fund children's hospitals. When the world thinks of the Church, they usually think, *Oh, those people just want your money.*

TRUE SERVANTHOOD CAN CHANGE THE WORLD'S PARADIGM

In our blindness to the needs around us, we have painted ourselves into the proverbial corner. It is time to come out and be what we are called and anointed to be: *servants.* True servanthood—servanthood in action—has the power to change the paradigm of how the world views us. Individuals and governments are not afraid to empower a servant, but they are afraid to empower anyone or anything that lords it over them. Few will ask the proud for help, but anyone will ask a servant for help.

We have been acting more like Saul the murderer than Paul the martyr. When Saul the persecutor, accuser and religious enforcer saw the light, he had a paradigm shift. He suddenly shifted his energies and loyalties. He began to preserve and protect the very people he once had tried to kill. A single dramatic encounter with the Prince of Peace transformed Saul, the thundering voice of religion, into Paul, the gentle servant voice of heaven.

DAVID SPEAKS

As Tommy explained, God changed Saul into Paul with a single supernatural encounter. Let me point out that God then sent this Jewish expert in the Law to devote his life to ministry among non-Jewish people. God knows our limitations, but He insists on using us in spite of them. Time and time again, He leads simple, ordinary people into impossible situations to open their eyes and ignite their hearts with compassion. Then He launches them armed with little more than His compassion and the promise that He will lead them and never forsake them.

Compassion is what landed me in southern Sudan, one of the driest and most desolate places on the planet. It all began after the Lord arranged for me to see several television reports on the plight of Sudanese refugees in squatter camps. Most of the people living in the southern half of Sudan were nominal Christians or animists. While they struggled to avoid death from starvation due to the ravages of drought and famine, Islamic rebels from the north targeted them for slaughter as infidels.

I began to pray about their situation, and as my compassion grew, so did my conviction that I was to take the cross and bowl to Sudan and minister to them in any way I could. I applied to the Sudanese government for an entry visa, but it was officially an Islamic state and I was a Christian. My application was blocked by bureaucracy and red tape at every turn.

Then God supernaturally released the finances and opened doors, so I could reach a tiny United Nations regional base near a place where the borders of Uganda, Kenya, Ethiopia and Sudan converge. Then I persuaded them to allow one of their charter flights to take me 400 miles to the tiny settlement of Waat, in southern Sudan.

My First View Caused a State of Shock for Two Weeks

As the plane touched down on the dusty little landing strip, billows of dust filled the air and hundreds of peasants converged on us. Some of the men helped us unload what seemed to be a meager handful of supplies, considering the desperate situation there. I didn't realize that I would encounter a scene that kept me in a state of shock for the next two weeks.

When I stepped from the plane, I saw the emaciated bodies of adult men and women, all of them without a stitch of clothing. They weren't nude by choice—they simply had no access to clothing, animal skins or even leaves of any kind to cover themselves.

What am I doing here? This is a holocaust! I thought as I stood there with the cross and bowl. I had washed the feet of thousands of people with those simple implements, but I felt utterly helpless at that bleak moment. As far as my eyes could see, I saw nothing but desperation and hopelessness.

I had been in wars and squatter camps before, and I had seen abject poverty throughout the world; but I had never encountered anything like this. My heart broke more and more with every step I took into the squatter's settlement.

I saw hundreds of children whose little legs looked like sticks attached to knees that resembled a man's knuckles. Malnutrition had reduced the bodies of children and adults alike into horrible stick-figure caricatures of the walking dead, and I won't even describe the details of what I saw in that place.

"Oh God, What Are We to Do?"

People lined up from before sunrise until midnight to lower their buckets into a single broken well for water. (I discovered later that the water from this well was contaminated because of the human waste that penetrated the soil.)

That night, my mind began to spin and I cried out, "Oh God, what are we to do?" The answer eluded me, so I closed my eyes and drifted

off into a fitful sleep. The next morning I rose earl
the area with local tribesmen to collect the dead. T
ally saw vultures waiting for the weakest people to
for them to feed on the bodies of the dead before t

I walked around in shock for the next few ꞈ_,
prayed in the Spirit. I was overwhelmed. It seemed hopelessly inadequate
for me to simply tell people that Jesus loved them and to wash their feet
when they were dying. God wanted me to do something more, but I
didn't know where to begin.

I befriended the locals, and I listened to their stories about loved
ones who had died. They knew very little, if anything, about the gospel.
They just knew that "Islam was bad and Christianity good." They told
me stories about Muslim soldiers who held people at gunpoint and said,
"If you convert to Islam, we will give you clothes and food. If you do not,
we will shoot you." Many had been shot. Every day I spent in Waat, I
asked God, "Where do I start?"

Two weeks later, I returned to South Africa and felt led to enlist the
assistance of 70 churches of different denominations. Then I returned to
Sudan with a group of farmers to acquire soil samples which were test-
ed in South African laboratories to determine what types of nutrients
were needed.

I contacted the United Nations, the South African Department of
Foreign Affairs and the South African Navy. By God's grace, they all
agreed to help. With the assistance of the South African Navy, we shipped
several tons of clothing and seed donated by the churches and the farmers to the port of Mombasa in Kenya. We then trucked it over 2,000 miles
of some of the worst roads on the planet to the United Nations' regional
center on the border. The United Nations agreed to fly the clothing and
the seed the last 400 miles to Waat, since there were no roads.

SERVANTS SEE NEEDS THROUGH JESUS' EYES

We began to teach the Sudanese refugees the basic truths of Christianity
and helped them raise up Christian leadership from among their own
ranks. I also took a team of South African volunteers to Waat and we

hoed 80 acres of ground and planted crops. Despite the difficul-
s, we managed to clothe 12,000 people. God let me see the desperate
need, and His compassion left me no choice. I shared the need with others and, as Christians, we could not go in and not be moved. *True servants
can't see a need through Jesus' eyes and remain unmoved.*

James the brother of Jesus said, "If a brother or sister is naked and
destitute of daily food, and one of you says to them, 'Depart in peace, be
warmed and filled,' but you do not give them the things which are needed for the body, what does it profit? Thus also faith by itself, if it does
not have works, is dead."[5]

God talks about a people who keep on looking but do not understand. Their ears are dull, their eyes are dim, and their hearts are insensitive. They *look but do not see.*[6]

The Lord continually works with us to help us see through His eyes
and view the world as servants. Precisely when God completes His character adjustments and produces repentance in our hearts, He once again
brings the unexpected into our lives to see how well we have learned the
lesson.

A PRAYER OF COMPLAINT
TEACHES A LESSON

Another time, while walking across the nation of South Africa, I offered
the Lord a "prayer of complaint" in my frustration one morning: "Lord,
where are all the opportunities out here?" (I don't know why I said that.
Hardly a day goes by on the road without something special taking
place.) The Lord began to speak to me through a passage in the book of
Isaiah:

> Hear, you deaf; and look, you blind, that you may see. Who is
> blind but My servant, or deaf as My messenger whom I send?
> Who is blind as he who is perfect, and blind as the LORD's ser-
> vant? Seeing many things, but you do not observe; opening the
> ears, but he does not hear.[7]

I asked God to forgive me for being so insensitive to all the divine opportunities I had missed, and my eyes fell on another verse in the same chapter of Isaiah:

> I will bring the blind by a way they did not know; I will lead them in paths they have not known. I will make darkness light before them, and crooked places straight. These things I will do for them, and not forsake them.[8]

I felt God's grace flood through me, but I would soon find out that the Lord intended to make sure I learned my lesson.

As I walked down the road that afternoon, I sensed a new spiritual sharpness I didn't have before. This was something new that I wanted to try out, so I did what I usually do while out in the country: I asked, "Lord, what are you doing out here today?"

LORD, I DON'T NEED TROUBLE TODAY

A highway patrol car drove past me a little later on. I watched as it slowed down to make a U-turn and then came back toward me. When the patrol car pulled off the road and onto the gravel berm in front of me, I thought, *Oh no! Lord, I don't need trouble today.*

Then I watched with growing concern as a very large provincial traffic officer unfolded himself from the car and walked toward me. He peered down at me (we were both standing) and asked, "What are you doing?"

"I'm walking to Cape Town," I replied, and he looked at me with a strange expression (probably because I was walking in almost the opposite direction from Cape Town). Then I told him about Jesus and how my love for Him had compelled me to walk across the southern continent of Africa, showing the servant love of Jesus to all I met.

I could see that he didn't understand what I was talking about, but he decided he liked me anyway. In fact, he evidently decided to adopt me as his personal project for the day. He squeezed back into his patrol car, turned it around and then announced that he was going to escort me to the next town!

It is strange enough to see me walking along with the cross, the bowl and the odd-looking water-tank contraption I use for my road ministry. My new friend added his own touch to the effect as he escorted me from the opposite side of the road in his highway patrol car with its blue lights flashing. All the while, the traffic officer hung out of his window and listened to me talk about Jesus in between the passing traffic.

While all of this was going on, I continued to silently ask the Lord, *What is going on out here? Are You doing anything here today?*

"No, I Am Riding with You!"

We didn't get very far before the highway patrol car began to overheat because of the slow pace, so I suggested to my escort that he drive ahead and wait for me at the crest of a distant hill I pointed out. He protested in Afrikaans,[9] *"Nee ek ry saam met jou!"* ("No, I am riding with you!")

We covered only a short distance before the driver of a small pickup truck jammed on his brakes and jumped out! It turned out that the man was a Christian, and he enthusiastically began to exchange stories with me while the highway patrolman hung even further out of his window to satisfy his growing curiosity.

Just before the man left, he laid his hands on me and prayed for me. Then he pulled out the equivalent of two $10 bills out of his pocket and stuck them in my hand before he left. Then I looked at my thoroughly confused semiofficial escort, stepped across the road and said, "Isn't God good?"

"Look," I continued, "the Lord wants to bless you with $10."

"I can't take your money," he protested. But when I assured him that God wanted to bless him, he reluctantly took the money. Once again we resumed our journey; and in spite of God's dealings with me that very morning, I again asked, *Lord, what is going on out here today?* (Obviously, I was still unaware of my spiritual blindness.)

Darkness began to close in on us and the officer insisted that I ride in his car so that I wouldn't get hit by passing traffic. He relented when I explained that the Lord had specifically instructed me to walk and not to accept a ride from anyone. I continued my trek into the evening hours with the flashing blue light piercing the darkness.

POLICE ESCORT ME HOME

My escort patiently and faithfully followed me all the way to the city limits of the town where our camping trailer was parked. At the outskirts of the town, I finally agreed to ride with my new friend and I let him load up my gear. Then he turned on his flashing pursuit lights and let his siren wail loud enough to wake the whole town. He drove me through town with great delight, hurtling around the corners on two wheels and rushing me back to my trailer in a classic Hollywood-style police chase. I hung on for dear life, but I was still asking, *Lord, what's going on out here today?*

I wish I had a picture of Carol's expression when we screeched to a halt in front of our trailer, with flashing lights and screaming siren. She thought I'd been arrested! Only then did it dawn on me what God had tried to show me all day; I was right in the *middle* of what God was doing. Once more He had extended His grace to me in the midst of my insensitivity to His Spirit.

We invited the traffic officer into the trailer and told him about the redeeming love of Jesus. He suddenly became quiet and listened closely. He was beginning to realize what Jesus did for him on the cross.

Finally, he sat down outside our trailer door and placed his feet in the bowl with the humility of a child. It was a study in contrast, because under any other circumstances the officer's uniform and great size would have been intimidating.

He quietly received Jesus as his Lord and Savior and said he had battled alcoholism all of his life. We cast out the spirit of alcoholism in the name of Jesus, and we watched him drive off into the distance.

A Sequel Comes Out of Nowhere

The story had a beautiful sequel nearly two years and 1,200 miles later. As I left one town and headed toward another town called Mossel Bay in the southern part of South Africa, a car seemed to come out of nowhere and pulled up next to me. I instantly noticed the red stripes, blue star and blue light of a Cape Provincial Highway Patrol car.

Then the driver leaned out of the car and asked, "You don't remember me?" My heart leapt with joy. "Of course I remember you! Your name is Danie. You are world famous. I've told people about you in different parts of the world." He climbed out of his car and ran across the road to hug me with breathtaking enthusiasm.

I immediately asked him, "Are you still walking with the Lord?" He said yes and eagerly told me about the Lord's work in his life. He asked if I remembered casting the spirit of alcoholism out of him, and then he said he had been totally delivered! It turned out that he was a member of the church in Mossel Bay where I was to speak the following evening.

The next night, as I entered the church, I saw Danie and his wife sitting in the packed congregation. I knew the conversion testimony about Danie that I had shared around the world would face its greatest test right there in his home church.

The Congregation Roared with Laughter

I told the story exactly as I always did, complete with all the graphic detail and humor. The congregation roared with laughter as the story unfolded, and no one suspected that the main character in the story sat among them.

I watched Danie and his wife clap and rock with laughter as I shared point after point, and Danie often nodded his head in acknowledgment. The broad grin on his face only spurred me on. When I described how he surrendered his life to the Lord and cast out the spirit of alcoholism, the congregation was visibly moved.

Then I leaned forward and said, "He is with us tonight! His name is Danie, and he's sitting right there." The congregation instantly erupted in sustained applause and thanksgiving to God. (I can't help but think to myself, *Lord, I'm sure glad that one of us knew what You were doing out in the country two years ago.*)

We all tend to look at things through our natural, rather than our supernatural, eyes. I call those supernatural eyes "Jesus eyes," and I pray that I will use His eyes more and more with each new day.

VIEW THE WORLD AS JESUS DID

The Word of God reveals the way Jesus looked at people, cities and nations: with compassionate eyes. Luke's Gospel tells us that as Jesus approached Jerusalem and *saw* the city, he began to *weep* over it.[10] Sometimes the ministry of servanthood causes you to see something that moves you to tears.

Another time, Mary and Martha sent a message to Jesus that their brother, Lazarus, was dying. Jesus purposely lingered until after Lazarus died; and when He eventually arrived, each of the sisters told Him, "Lord, if You had been here, my brother would not have died."[11]

Jesus knew He was sent from the Father, and He knew what He was about to do (raise Lazarus from the dead). Yet when Jesus arrived and *saw* the human sorrow created by death and loss in those He loved, He began to weep with them with such passion that the Jews who saw it said, "See how He loved him!"[12] When we look through the eyes of Jesus, we cannot remain unmoved.

Jesus also looked at people through eyes there were extraordinarily sensitive to

Compassion and sensitivity aren't enough for true servants; genuine love must bind them together and fuel physical acts of service under the guidance of the Holy Spirit.

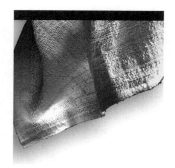

the hidden needs of people around Him. When a woman who was suffering from an incurable blood condition approached Jesus in the middle of a packed crowd, He sensed her touch and perceived her need. This is amazing, because Jesus was surrounded by a sea of people!

When Jesus *looked* at the woman, she trembled because she thought she had been "caught," but Jesus had something else in mind. He told her, "Daughter, be of good cheer; your faith has made you well. Go in peace."[13] *He looked with sensitive eyes* and said words of encouragement: "Take courage; be of good cheer."

Compassion and sensitivity aren't enough for true servants; genuine love must bind them together and fuel physical acts of service under the guidance of the Holy Spirit. Servant love is active love, and no one can resist love in action.

UP IS DOWN AND DOWN IS UP

Jesus warned us through His teachings that servant love is based on the up-is-down-and-down-is-up principle of promotion and power in God's kingdom. As we noted earlier, Jesus told His disciples, "Whoever desires to become *great* among you shall be your *servant*."[14]

The Lord's lifestyle was vivid proof that the way up is the way down. He washed His disciples' feet, helped fishermen pull in record harvests and served tens of thousands of people in healing, deliverance, teaching and even in supernaturally providing food. He went out of His way to raise Lazarus from the dead; he cooked breakfast for the disciples after a weary night's toil out on the water after His resurrection. He dared to challenge the full power of the Sanhedrin just to touch unclean lepers, forgive prostitutes, open blind eyes and restore withered arms. The list goes on and on.

Even though God called Carol and me to make a prophetic statement of His servant love, it is *in this very area* that He challenges me the most.

One winter morning I was walking through the beautiful sugarcane fields of Natal, South Africa, accompanied by a young man from Iceland. We noticed a stooped figure come into view in the distance. The figure, who appeared to be an elderly peasant man, used both hands to lean heavily on a tall stick as he hobbled down the road.

On that particular morning, I had my cross and bowl; but I accidentally left my towels behind for the first time, due to some minor complications. As we drew closer to the shuffling figure, we crossed the road to talk to the elderly man. To our surprise, he wasn't elderly at all. This Zulu[15] man was in his late 30s or early 40s, but when we glanced at his feet, we knew why he appeared to be so old.

He was trying to walk on the most tragic, blood-stained and leprous limbs I had ever seen. In a mixture of English and a few Zulu words, we asked the man where he was going; he told us in Zulu that he was going to Murchison.

Each Step Was Agony

There was a mission hospital in Murchison, but it was at least 12 miles from where we stood, and the road surface was incredibly rough. Each step the man took on his diseased and bleeding feet must have been agonizingly painful. The man said he had to walk because he couldn't afford to hire a taxi.

Normally I do not carry money with me on the road, but I put my hand in my pocket and found to my surprise that I had the exact amount the man needed for the taxi fare. I put the money in his hand and turned to continue my journey. *After all,* I told myself, *I can't minister to him any further because I did not have my towels with me.* We said good-bye and walked away, but I hadn't gone more than about 10 paces when I heard a small voice within me say, "You have grieved Me; you did not wash his feet, nor did you show him My servant love."

I quickly retraced my steps and put the cross on the ground. I opened the tap on my water tanks and began to fill the bowl and helped him settle into my little folding chair. I can still remember the bite of the chilly winter breeze blowing across my arms and the back of my neck.

As my young Icelandic companion looked on, I said, "I don't know if we could ever explain to him what we are about to do. We will just have to trust the Holy Spirit to show him." Then I picked up the bleeding, broken feet before me and placed them gently in the bowl. As I washed and soothed that man's leprous feet, I could feel hot tears welling up in my eyes as I asked the Lord to help him understand His comforting, serving love.

"TAKE OFF YOUR SHIRT AND DRY HIS FEET"

As I finished, I cried out in a desperate but silent prayer, *Lord, we now have no way to dry his feet!* Then I sensed the Holy Spirit say, "Take off your shirt and dry his feet."

I took off my T-shirt and used it to gently dab his feet. Blood and mucous had soaked into the fabric by the time the man's feet were totally dry, but somehow I knew Jesus would have done at least this much and more. Then we said good-bye once more and resumed our walk. As I carried the bloodied shirt in my hand, I was keenly aware that I would feel the bite of the freezing wind for the rest of the day. That night I sensed the Holy Spirit say to me, "Flesh and blood will not reveal this to him but your Father who is in heaven. As you have done it unto the least of these, you have done it unto Me."

I managed to hear God that time, but there have been other times when I was insensitive to His gentle voice and I simply missed it. Carol and I live in a beautiful area of Port Elizabeth, a seaside city. We can see around the bay for about 20 miles from our home, and we are only 700 yards from the beach. In the middle of the road to the beachfront there is a grassy strip dividing the traffic flow in opposite directions. That road intersects with the beach road at a traffic light.

Some time ago, a young homeless man started camping on the traffic island by the traffic light. At first he was fairly presentable; but as time went on his appearance deteriorated markedly, he grew a big beard, and his hair became matted.

"JUST BRING HIM BACK"

One day I passed by this man on the traffic island and I sensed the Lord saying, "Tonight, when Carol puts your dinner on the table, *take it to him.*" When I reached the traffic island that evening, the man was gone and I never saw him again. I asked God, "Please help me. Just bring him back." Sadly, I learned a few weeks later that someone had fatally shot that young man right there on the traffic island in the middle of the road. Many times since then, I have asked God to help me because sometimes I simply miss it.

Whose eyes do you use when you go into work each day? Do you walk inside the office or plant and simply greet "old Pete" who's been there for 20 years and Mary who's been there for 15? Do you just say "Hi" or do you look at them with the supernatural eyesight of Jesus Christ?

Continually pray that God will change your heart and He will. When God first called me to carry the cross and bowl, I wasn't much of a weeper. In fact, I almost never cried (now I cry all the time). For 14 months during that early period, God spoke to me every day and He did something to my heart. I couldn't even watch the evening news without weeping! I even wept when I drove my car. It became so common that Carol used to say, "Well, there he goes again."

Jesus was breaking my heart and changing me so that I could begin to see with His eyes and serve with His servant heart. Allow Him to do the same for you. *When you touch the Lord in the throne room of intimacy, your faith is transformed into servanthood.* It is there that He transforms and prepares you to become a carrier of His servant love. Allow Him to adorn you with servant eyes in the well of intimacy.

Notes

1. Please understand that I am *not* proposing that Jesus came *only* to give us an eye-opening experience or to simply change our way of thinking. These things are important, particularly in the context of developing a servant heart; yet they are only incidental or in addition to His central purpose: to lay down His life as the sacrificed Lamb of God who would take away the sin of the world.
2. John 4:35.
3. See Acts 3; 4.
4. Hebrews 12:2.
5. James 2:15-17.
6. See Isaiah 6:9.

7. Isaiah 42:18-20.
8. Isaiah 42:16.
9. Afrikaans is one of the official languages of the Republic of South Africa. It was developed from the Dutch language in the seventeenth century.
10. See Luke 19:41.
11. John 11:21,32.
12. John 11:36.
13. Luke 8:48.
14. Mark 10:43, italics mine.
15. This man was a member of the Zulu tribe. In the 1800s, the Zulu nation challenged the might of the British Empire. The Zulu were once Africa's most feared warriors.

CHAPTER EIGHT

LISTENING WITH YOUR EYES
AND SEEING WITH YOUR EARS

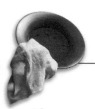

If your car was manufactured any time after the fall of the Berlin Wall, you automatically assume that when tune-up time comes around, that your dealer will plug your car into one of those electronic machines for electronic analysis and troubleshooting.

Things work differently in the off-track pit area of a professional racing track. You might see some of those tune-up units there, but they are rarely hooked up to the custom-built, cutting-edge machines that power grand prix and stock race cars. Skilled mechanics personally tune those cars by using their *ears* to "see" into the internal workings of the engines they build. They "hear" by watching the engine operations, rhythms and timing marks as the engines run at various speeds.

A skilled pit mechanic can listen to a race car roar past and then tell you the exact make and size of the engine under the hood—even if his back is facing the racetrack. It is all a matter of listening with your eyes and seeing with your ears.

We all come into this world with the same basic equipment package. What sets us apart from one another is how we use what we have been given. Our encounter with the Servant of God should permanently change the way we use our equipment package. The first things we should throw out are our *assumptions* about people based on stereotypes and public opinion. God wants us to listen with our eyes and see with our ears.

A SEVERELY HEIGHT-CHALLENGED SOCIAL OUTCAST ACQUIRES A HOUSEGUEST

That reminds me of the senior agent at a large tax office who was a known crook and one of the wealthiest people in his city. He always dressed in the best of the best, but it didn't help him overcome his condition as a severely height-challenged man and an absolute social outcast. He had one of the nicest homes in the region, but no one wanted to visit there.

When a well-known preacher came to town, a lot of the townspeople showed up to greet him. In all of the excitement, a spontaneous street party was born. Meanwhile, the wealthy height-challenged tax agent decided he would see this man at any cost. He knew he had no chance in the swirling crowd for at least two reasons: first, he was short ("height-challenged" for the politically correct crowd); and second, he was the tax agent everyone loved to hate.

His Plan B was unorthodox but successful. He anticipated where the informal parade would go and climbed a certain sycamore tree that overhung most of the road. Sure enough, the crowd surged into the narrow street below him, and finally the preacher came into view.

I would give anything to meet him, the man thought to himself as the preacher drew nearer. *The first thing I would do is invite him to my house . . . even though I know he wouldn't come.*

Suddenly the evangelist looked up for some reason just as he reached the spot beneath the tax agent's location in the tree. Then he said the most amazing thing: "Zacchaeus, make haste and come down, for *today I must stay at your house.*"[1]

THE CROWD PARTED, SO THE TAX MAN COULD REACH JESUS

The street party nearly ground to a halt when the townspeople heard what the preacher said. Zacchaeus nearly fell off the tree branch in shock, but he quickly climbed down from his perch, and the crowd parted in amazement so that the tax man could reach Jesus in the middle of the street. The crowd reaction was immediate. "He has gone to be a guest *with a man who is a sinner.*"[2] They couldn't believe this holy man could stoop so low. It was illegal for someone who was so upright to associate with someone who was so low down!

Zacchaeus had his own response to Jesus' words: "**Look,** Lord, I give *half of my goods* to the poor; and if I have taken anything from anyone by false accusation, *I restore fourfold.*"[3] The Master had only said He wanted to come to dinner, and this man vowed in front of his enemies that he was giving away half of all he owned and would repay those he'd cheated at a rate far beyond what the law required.

When Jesus looked at Zacchaeus in the tree, He *saw* a man with a big heart who was hungry for God. Everyone else saw a crook with a covetous heart who would do anything for recognition, power and acceptance.

When the people heard Zacchaeus say he would give away money and repay those he cheated, they thought, *There he goes again. That social outcast is trying to impress Jesus for his own gain.* Jesus heard the fruits of genuine repentance and said:

> *Today salvation has come to this house, because he also is a son of Abraham; for the Son of Man has come to seek and to save that which was lost.*[4]

ZACCHAEUS DESPERATELY WANTED GOD

Prevailing public opinion held that Zacchaeus was a social outcast who got rich by taking from others; Jesus saw an outcast from heaven who desperately wanted to find God—even if it meant losing everything he owned on Earth.

Something happened that day in Jericho, which I described in my book *God's Dream Team*:

> When a recipe is created, there is often a single *catalytic* ingredient. A catalyst is something that triggers or initiates significant change when it comes into contact with other things. If that particular catalytic ingredient is missing from the recipe, then the whole cake collapses. I remember that when my sister was first learning to cook, she failed to understand the difference between baking soda and baking powder. For the uninitiated, it

is more than mere semantics. It is the difference between a cake rising as it should, filling the house with its flavorful aroma as it bakes, or one that smells good, but doesn't look or taste as it should. *One ingredient can make the difference* between success and failure, between victory and defeat.[5]

By listening with His eyes and seeing with His ears, Jesus looked beyond the obvious to accurately perceive the longing of Zacchaeus's heart. When He invited Himself to dinner, that became the catalyst that released hope, faith and salvation to Zacchaeus, the social outcast and known crook.

Jesus gave you and me the same anointing and responsibility He demonstrated with Zacchaeus in Jericho. As true servants of God, it is time for us to listen and see in a new way.

D A V I D   S P E A K S

A TRUE SERVANT DISCERNS THAT WHICH ISN'T OBVIOUS

Tommy's description of the situation with Zacchaeus illustrates an important point: The inconspicuous and the unseen are sometimes more important than the obvious. The problem is that the inconspicuous and the unseen must be perceived from a different angle, using our senses in fresh ways as the Holy Spirit directs us. *One of the major dimensions of a true servant heart is being able to discern that which is not obvious.*

Discernment is one of the most important gifts God gives us as His children. The Bible says, "But you have an anointing from the Holy One, and you know all things."[6] Discernment has been my vital "companion" over the years in my dealings with both church leaders and people on the streets. I've learned that discernment is especially important when I approach towns or cities for the first time when I am ministering on the road.

I and two companions were on a long and hot ministry walk. We were between Victoria Falls and Lusaka in Zambia, Africa, and it was starting to get dark as we approached a tiny village. The village inhabitants were busily preparing for nightfall by gathering wood and water for their fires before the last light disappeared.

When I entered the village, the first thing I discerned was the presence of a prevailing spirit of religion. It seemed strange to me because there were no great religious centers, worship structures or overtly occult symbols in the village. Nevertheless, I had a nagging impression, or suspicion, in my spirit that whatever brand of religious spirit dwelt in the village, it was out of touch with real Christianity.

Our first task was to find a suitable place to sleep. There was a police station in the village, but such stations in most small Zambian villages like this one had "police clubs" attached to them. These clubs are nothing more than degenerate drinking halls that attract all kinds of activity, which makes it unwise to camp near them. We quickly realized we couldn't spend the night in the village, and that was a hard fact to accept after such a long, tiring day.

Then, to our delight, we spotted a tiny church building with a house attached. There was a large fence around the property, but the sign at the gate reassured us it was a Christian ministry. I walked up to the main house and knocked on the door. When two white people greeted me, I introduced myself and explained what I was doing. I reassured them that our goal was to help them build the kingdom of God in the area. Then I asked permission for us to camp at the bottom of the property and told them we would not ask for anything or inconvenience them in any way.

One of the major dimensions of a true servant heart is being able to discern that which is not obvious.

"THERE'S NO ROOM FOR YOU HERE"

After a 15-second pause, I was told, *"No, you are not one of us. There's no room for you here.*" I couldn't believe what I had just heard. I returned to my two companions with tears welling up in my eyes, and we quietly left the village and spent the night in the bush.

I couldn't help but ponder Jesus' admonition to "keep through Your name those whom You have given Me, that they may be one as We are."[7] Unfortunately, I had discerned correctly. The village was marked by religious spirits rather than by Kingdom hearts.

Oddly enough, we received the opposite treatment in the next village the following night. This village had a different personality and spirit about it. It was the same size as the previous village, and I could tell that one man seemed to dominate everything in that tiny town.

We soon met "Johnny the Greek," the man who owned the liquor store, the butchery, the service station and the local general dealer's store. It was evident that Johnny wasn't a believer, but I explained to him what we were doing and asked if he could find us a safe place to sleep for the night.

"I'VE GOT JUST THE PLACE"

"Sure," he said. "You are preaching the Word of God; I've got just the place." We scurried after him as he led us down to the local scrap yard (it was his of course). Johnny the Greek unlocked two huge steel gates, each as high as the 10-foot wall around it—a wall with large pieces of broken glass embedded in the concrete around the top.

With a smile he ushered us in and assured us that he would return the following morning. Then he locked the gates and disappeared. That evening, I sat on the roof of one of the wrecked cars and smiled as I thought to myself, *Well, Dave Cape, you mighty man of power for the hour, you finally landed here in a scrap yard, ministering to motor wrecks.*

The reality saddened me. The "Christians" we met the night before rejected us, but this unsaved man took us in. I thought of the Scripture verse from John's third epistle:

Beloved, you do faithfully whatever you do for the brethren and for strangers, who have borne witness of your love before the church. If you send them forward on their journey in a manner worthy of God, you will do well.[8]

Discernment always serves as a great ally and protector, no matter where or how we serve in God's kingdom. Wisdom is its close companion. It sits alongside and crowns discernment. This combination is vital in the areas of giving and counseling—two areas of service available to nearly every Christian, at one level or another.

My wife, Carol, has a generous, giving nature; and she has discovered the truth that we cannot outgive God. However, she acquired hard-won wisdom in her giving when she sowed monetary gifts into the financial needs of others, based on her compassion alone. She discovered that in some cases, individuals created their own financial crises because they failed to learn biblical lessons on stewardship.

THE LEAKY FINANCIAL BUCKETS OF POOR STEWARDS

When other Christians generously but blindly refill the leaky financial buckets of poor, unwise or lazy stewards, they can actually circumvent God's purposes in their lives. God wants us to give generously in establishing His kingdom, but He doesn't condone our hasty decisions to throw His finances into a bottomless pit. Once again, it pays to look beyond the obvious when serving.

Some people can give the appearance that life is going well and they have no need of anything. Then one day you learn that their lives have caved in. *The truth is often found in what people don't say as much as in what they do say.*

Some years ago, Carol and I hosted a marriage enrichment course. A dear couple came to our home to participate in the course, but on the first night, the young lady proudly declared that she and her husband had no need for such a course because they had "a superior marriage." By the time we reached the end of the course, their marriage fell apart through a bizarre set of circumstances and they were divorced just two months later. We should have been listening to what this young bride did *not* say as much as to what she did say.

The prophet Isaiah prophesied of Jesus, "He shall not judge by the sight of His eyes, nor decide by the hearing of His ears."[9] Anyone who steps out by faith to do God's will must personally learn how to hear and trust Him. It is good to seek wise counsel, but in the end the decision you make is between you and God.

THE LORD CHALLENGED US TO LIVE BY FAITH

Many years ago, when Carol and I left the pastoral ministry to carry the cross and bowl, we felt the Lord challenge us to live by faith. Our church sent us out with the best intentions and offered to continue paying our salary to us, but Carol and I knew the church's finances would not stretch that far.

At the same time, Carol and I each received revelation from the Lord based on the Scripture verse "The just shall live by faith."[10] We both felt that this word applied to every area of our lives. Finances were extremely tight at that stage, and our ministry did not have the public profile we now enjoy.

When we sought the counsel of two men with established ministries, they gave us conflicting advice. One said, "Always present your needs up front and make them as widely known as possible. This allows people to pray for your needs and to be open to the prompting of the Lord to sow into your lives." The second man said, "Never tell anyone about a single need. Even if you are living on bread and water, keep it to yourself. If anyone asks, say you are doing fine."

In the end, we decided to simply trust God to speak to *discerning* Christians about our unpublished needs as they occurred or to meet them by other means if necessary. More than a decade later, Carol and I can tell you that God has supplied all our needs "according to His riches in glory," just as His Word declares.[11]

THE IMPORTANT THINGS WE DO NOT SEE

Have you ever examined a house that someone spruced up to be sold? More accurately, have you seen a house somebody patched up just enough to *look* better than it really was? The seller hopes that potential buyers won't ask what is underneath.

Perhaps the owners removed all the mildew and rotted plaster and replaced it with fresh layers of plaster to conceal the original problems. They filled the growing cracks in the walls and foundation with putty and then painted over them. Questionable plumbing received a liberal dose of drain cleaner, and leaky pipes were hastily wrapped or concealed just long enough for potential buyers to pass through.

Of course, you can count on the sellers to prepare their garden, fertilize and trim the lawn, and make sure the flowers are in full bloom. Everything may look fine to the human eye, but once the new tenants move in and try to hang their first picture, they may discover the wall is actually hollow when a big chunk of plaster falls out of the wall. Then comes the wood rot under the carpet, and the sorry tale goes on.

Sometimes we see things in people's lives only after they begin serving, which makes it vital that we learn to look through and beyond surface appearances. Jesus' words to Thomas the disciple applauded those whose faith goes beyond the natural observance of the eye. He said, "Thomas, because you have seen Me, you have believed. Blessed are those who *have not seen* and yet have believed."[12]

Tommy and I each have the opportunity to visit many different churches around the world in the course of ministry. It usually doesn't take very long for us to figure out exactly what is going on after we walk into a church. Our first impression may be that everything is excellent and running fine, but then we learn later of severe problems.

If the Heart Is Bad, the Body Is at Risk

Healthy churches are like healthy human bodies: If the heart of the church is full of the life of God, then it will affect the health and appearance of the whole body. If the heart is bad, it puts the rest of the body at risk (both the seen and the unseen).

We are *not* knocking excellence. We believe that Jesus is a savior of great excellence. However, there is a great difference between excellence and perfection. *Perfection is law; excellence is grace.*

Some years ago, when I was in Israel, I came upon a Bedouin shepherd working with his sheep. I was struck by the unique way he worked with his sheep. In Western nations, shepherds tend to walk behind their sheep and herd them with the assistance of sheepdogs that respond to the blow of a whistle.

This Bedouin shepherd used the same methods described thousands of years ago in the Bible. A Middle Eastern shepherd walks ahead of his sheep, and the sheep follow as he calls. This is why Jesus told His Middle Eastern followers, "My sheep *hear My voice*, and I know them, and they *follow* Me."[13]

CHURCHES THAT PATCH UP THE CRACKS TO PUT ON A GOOD SHOW

I believe that many fine churches lost members because the pastors often drove the sheep rather than allowing themselves to be model Hebrew shepherds who led by example and nurtured through love more than fear. Some churches patch up their cracks and mildewed dark corners just enough to look good on the surface.[14] If you begin to scratch at the thin veneer of the surface, you will find members who are weary and stumbling from being driven. It is not what we see but what we don't see that really matters.

Some people in local churches may appear not to have any needs. They may serve and entertain friends and strangers alike with grace and excellence. Their children may seem to do and say all the right things, and their notes and phone calls of encouragement are always on time.

We know a very successful couple who have giving hearts. Their generosity and hospitality extend beyond what you ordinarily find. They faithfully comfort the hurting and offer hospitality to passersby. In their home they often host dinners to honor friends or faithful believers with fine cuisine and gracious fellowship in the Lord.

However, this couple confided to Carol and me that they were surprised no one in their church had ever invited them to their home. They were puzzled as to why no one ever reached out to them, even though they did not expect it.

Some people may feel that they can't match the standard of this dear couple. Others, on the other hand, may feel that this couple has it so together that they do not need to be invited anywhere.

On the surface, it may seem like this couple does not have a need, but their heart's desire is to be able to respond in a natural way to natural friendship with those around them. Once again, *it's not so much what we see but what we don't see.* Stay alert and quickly respond to the prompting of the Holy Spirit. Listen with your eyes and see with your ears.

HURTS AND WOUNDS THAT DEFY DETECTION

At times, the well-being of those we serve may hinge on our ability to accurately discern needs, hurts and wounds that defy detection through the normal use of our eyes and ears. Far too often, Christians find themselves trapped because they get themselves into situations and immediately click into the natural rather than the supernatural. We must *not* decide a course of action solely by what our eyes see or our ears hear.

One time, Carol and I visited a woman's home at the request of a mutual friend. A beautifully dressed lady greeted us at the door, and it was apparent that she was very refined. As we entered the home, we heard praise music wafting from a stereo system. She brought in her finest china to serve us tea and cake in classic South African tradition, and everything she did was gracious.

I thought to myself, *This is amazing!* Then the Holy Spirit began to prompt me with the warning "There is something wrong here." Then I realized that everything seemed just too perfect.

"Excuse me, ma'am, how is it with your husband?" I asked.

"Oh, my husband? He was baptized in the Jordan River."

LISTENING WITH YOUR EYES AND SEEING WITH YOUR EARS 127

I thought to myself, *Goodness me, am I missing it today, or what?*

We continued to drink tea with the praise music filling the house with melody; but a while later I again asked our gracious hostess, "Excuse me, ma'am, how is it with your husband now?"

This time, tears began to run down her cheeks and she said, "We've been separated for a long time, and we just got back together."

Gently, I said, "And it's not going well, is it?"

She nodded and admitted that I was right, and we began to minister to her in depth.

Carol and I could have just walked in there and said, "Wow! This woman is a spiritual giant"; but we would have totally missed what was taking place. We chose instead not to look at what our eyes saw or decide by what our ears heard.

Looking Beyond the Natural to the Supernatural

The routine patterns and appearances of life in the natural can lull us to sleep and blind us to the supernatural opportunities and provision of God. We overcome these obstacles to discernment by *looking through the natural to the supernatural.* People who learn to do this can change the course of history.

You and I cannot afford to go through the motions. Every day is a day of destiny for those who are determined to look through and beyond the natural to touch the supernatural plan of God for their lives.

Notes
1. Luke 19:5, italics mine.
2. Luke 19:7, italics mine.
3. Luke 19:8, italics mine.
4. Luke 19:9,10, italics mine.
5. Tommy Tenney, *God's Dream Team: A Call to Unity* (Ventura, CA: Regal Books, 1999), p. 126.
6. 1 John 2:20.

7. John 17:11.
8. 3 John 1:5,6.
9. Isaiah 11:3.
10. "The just shall live by faith" is quoted or mentioned four times in the Old and New Testaments: Habakkuk 2:4; Romans 1:17; Galatians 3:11; Hebrews 10:38. Romans 3:26 expresses the same idea.
11. Philippians 4:19.
12. John 20:29, italics mine.
13. John 10:27, italics mine.
14. Tommy Tenney deals more extensively with the problem of "concealed cracks" of disunity in churches and ministries and how they are repaired in *God's Dream Team: A Call to Unity*, pp. 88, 89.

CHAPTER NINE

TURNING DISAPPOINTMENT
INTO A *GOD* APPOINTMENT

Great people of God have a knack for turning their *disappointments into divine appointments*. These are the people whose names seem familiar to us today although they died hundreds or even thousands of years ago.

Moses totally and completely failed as a deliverer the first time around. His idea of deliverance was to kill an Egyptian he saw mistreat a Hebrew slave. His error and sin made him both an outlaw to his adoptive family in Pharaoh's house and a dangerous outsider to his native Hebrew people.

By all appearances, Moses aborted his destiny by committing murder, because he spent the next 40 years on the back side of the Sinai desert. A supernatural encounter with God, however, changed his disappointment into a divine appointment, and Moses demonstrated a faithfulness to his new call in God that helped him defy the might of Pharaoh and change the course of history.

Peter was the first disciple to recognize the deity of Christ and the only man that we know of in the Bible, apart from Jesus, to successfully walk on water. Yet he openly and boldly betrayed his Lord in the court-yard of the high priest in Jerusalem and wept as bitterly as the Lord's other betrayer, Judas Iscariot.

What set Peter apart from Judas? Both men betrayed Christ: Judas in secret and Peter in public. One hung himself from a lonely tree and the other went on to preach the first sermon in Church history before thousands of devout Jews in Jerusalem's crowded streets on its highest holy day.

The enemy tried to "sift" Peter by using his prideful failures against him, but Peter looked beyond his failure and betrayal to Jesus; and the Lord transformed his disappointment into a "God appointment." It changed Peter's life and set in motion the birth of the Church on the day of Pentecost.

Satan leveraged Judas's insecurities and greed in an attempt to abort the mission of Jesus and the birth of the Church, but he failed. It appears that Judas felt remorse over his betrayal of Jesus, but the Bible does not tell us he repented or asked Jesus for forgiveness. In the end, he took his own life and died in sin and shame.

On the other hand, Peter sought the face of God in the face of his own failures. His God appointment with the resurrected Christ so changed him that, according to Church history, Peter died for Christ through crucifixion on a cross. According to tradition, however, Peter felt he was unworthy to die exactly as his Master had died, so he had his executioners crucify him upside down.

Peter remained faithful to his Lord, even after he had failed. By God's grace, Peter's faithfulness altered his destiny and changed his disappointment into a divine appointment.

FAITHFULNESS IS LIKE GLUE

Faithfulness causes us to stick to our relationships, purposes, commitments and difficult tasks in spite of obstacles, doubt or adverse circumstances. We all want to hear God say to us one day, "Well done, good and faithful servant."[1] However, He won't say *"well done"* if you haven't done well. He won't say *"faithful"* if you have been unfaithful; nor will He call you *"servant"* if you have acted like an arrogant lord. His words will be the ultimate truth on that day.

You will need the glue of faithfulness if God assigns you to love someone who is unlovable, in order to win them over through your servanthood. It takes *faithfulness* to successfully use your servant's towel as a weapon when those you serve reject you again and again. In his book *Our Mission*, my friend Gene Edwards describes what God is looking for in servants and how they should respond to unfair treatment:

Let me give you a real tough test and see if you can pass it. Let's imagine that you have a dear friend, a Christian. Let's also imagine that something comes between the two of you. He does something toward you that is very un-Christian. He does something that a lost man would not even do. . . . The situation is so bad, and so unfair, that you know you would be justified in whatever you did.

You take it for a while; you're kind, you're nice. You do all the religious and spiritual things. Then a brand-new report comes in. He's up to even worse. Let me give you some idea of just what he might do. You've been lied about. You've suffered loss. Your friends no longer believe in you. . . . You've been called a liar, a cheat, a heretic, a cultist, a servant of Satan, a false prophet and a Judas. All this by a man who once called you friend. . . .

In the midst of all that, take a moment and stop. Get your emotions together. Don't start thinking ill of that man. Don't start listening to the little man inside of you. Instead, for a moment, walk up to the mountain and look through the eyes of Jesus Christ. Go get the heavenly view (the view *no man* in a crisis *ever* dares admit about his opponent). What is *His* viewpoint? It might amaze you . . . Jesus Christ is not offended with that brother. You may be, but the Lord is not. The Lord has not called down plagues on that man. The Lord has not decided to damn him to hell. The Lord is still kind. The Lord is still working in that man's life, trying to lead him further and deeper. . . .

If that is what the Lord is doing, then what shall *you* do? At this black moment, everything in your life is being ripped from under you. How shall you respond? Shall you respond with less than Christ? Remember, Christ is all you need. Remember, Christ is all you want. And thus, Christ is all you should get. The Lord has lacked a people who will walk to a mountain and see things from *His* view.[2]

It takes the glue of faithfulness to remain loyal to a difficult spouse, a terminally ill parent, an employer, a spiritual leader or a group of people that constantly knock you down with their cruel words, angry betrayals or delirious rantings. It is faithfulness that helps servants to get back up after being knocked down. Dave Cape knows how it feels to be cursed and spat upon, but faithfulness compels him to wipe his face with the towel of servanthood and extend his bowl and cross once again to friend and foe alike.

GET UP AND WIN!

No matter how many times you get knocked down on your journey of servanthood, if faithfulness helps you stick to your purpose and get back up one more time, then you have won! This ingredient of servanthood is a mandatory requirement for successful leadership in the Church.

I heard the late Jamie Buckingham say one time, "I've decided to stop picking up disappointed leaders, because by the definition, if they are leaders and if I have to pick them up and remotivate them, then they are not going to make it. They have to get up themselves and stick to the purpose of what they are called to do."

The "letter of the law" can only create a binding legal document; it is the faithfulness and loyalty of love that holds a marriage together. Most couples who have been married for 20 years or more will tell you they are closer today than they were the day they said "I do." They have survived the pressures of disappointment and the inevitable failure two human beings will experience in a marriage relationship. They have applied the glue of faithfulness and loyalty and allowed the pressure of adversity to bond them even closer together.

If you are faithful, then the disappointments you experience provide the pressure needed to connect you to a divine appointment and "glue" you to God.

Faithfulness and loyalty to a marriage commitment hold two partners to the purpose of their union long enough for the glue of God to make them one. It works the same way in the Church, which is a hodgepodge of radically different people all lumped together in one supernatural organism bound together by God's love. We need faithfulness to hold us together in Christ as we sharpen one another "as iron sharpens iron."[3] In the end, the fire and grace of God make us one and glorify the One who did it all.

God has called us to serve our families, our churches, our neighbors and the lost at home and even abroad. Remember that if you are *faithful,* then the disappointments you experience along the way *simply provide the pressure needed* to connect you to a divine appointment and "glue" you to God. Like a craftsman might press and clamp two pieces of splintered wood together until the glue dries and unites them in a permanent bond, God is applying relentless pressure to the Church to reunite its many splintered members in the bond of love.

The last apostle, Matthias, was not chosen for his preaching ability, mighty miracles, insightful teachings or prophetic prowess. Judas's replacement was chosen because of his *faithfulness.* He hung in there, no matter what kind of controversy swirled around Jesus or the fledgling Church. Peter said that Matthias and Joseph called Barsabas (the other candidate) "accompanied us all the time that the Lord Jesus went in and out among us, beginning from the baptism of John to that day when He was taken up from us."[4] Matthias was, above all, a *faithful* witness and servant of Christ.

In the scenario of our faithfulness to a faithful God, *retreat is not defeat and failure is not forever.* They are simply opportunities for God's strength to be revealed through our weaknesses[5] and for our disappointments to become divine appointments that bind us to Him.

DAVID SPEAKS

FAITHFULNESS MAKES THE ORDINARY GREAT

"Great people," in Tommy's words, "have a knack for turning their disappointments into divine appointments." You might be thinking, *What about ordinary people who work a factory job or sit in the same pew or seat at church every weekend?* Every person Tommy mentioned was an "ordinary" person. Their *faithfulness* made them "great." If you classify yourself as ordinary, that simply means that you are a candidate for greatness through faithfulness.

There are two good reasons why we must understand and operate in faithfulness as Christians. Two Scripture passages sum them up:

[Jesus said,] "In the world you will have tribulation; but be of good cheer, I have overcome the world."[6]

[Paul said,] "Moreover it is required in stewards that one be found faithful."[7]

Trouble and disappointment are sure things in life; and since every Christian is called to take up the towel of servanthood (this may also be read as stewardship), then every Christian is required to be faithful.

If we can learn God's way to deal with disappointment when it comes, then our disappointments can be transformed into divine appointments and victories. Satan does everything he can to turn our divine appointments into disheartening disappointments so that he can steal our joy, because he knows that "the joy of the LORD is [our] strength."[8] Disappointment is difficult to handle, particularly when you are serving others. When you are disappointed, there are at least three important things you must do: *make right choices, persevere for a purpose and respond rather than react.*

MAKE RIGHT CHOICES

Jacob, also known as Israel, is one of the three great patriarchs honored by Christians, Jews and Muslims alike. He didn't begin his life as a great person; he entered the world with the name of "Trickster" because of his scheming ways. Twice he cheated his older brother, Esau, and stole both his birthright and his inheritance. As a result, Jacob's father and mother sent him away to his uncle's home in Padan Aram to find a wife (and avoid the murderous anger of Esau).[9]

En route to his uncle's house, Jacob had his first encounter with the living God. It affected him so powerfully that he made a covenant to serve God and tithe a tenth of all he owned. In return, he wanted the

Lord to get him out of his mess with Esau.[10]

Then Jacob made his way to the sheep pastures of his uncle Laban and fell in love at first sight with his younger daughter, Rachel. Laban gladly took in his young nephew and asked him what he wanted for wages in return for his labor. Jacob quickly said he would serve his uncle for seven years if he could marry Rachel.[11]

Jacob served his uncle faithfully for seven years, and his love for Rachel made the time seem like a matter of days. Unfortunately, disappointment awaited him.

On the wedding night, Laban somehow managed to switch the sisters and Jacob spent his wedding night with Laban's oldest daughter, Leah. The following morning, a disappointed Jacob confronted his uncle only to be told that local custom demanded that the eldest daughter be married first. Laban softened the blow by slyly saying that Jacob could have Rachel as well if he served *another* seven years.[12]

Jacob had been tricked, abused and misused; and he had every right to be disappointed in the natural. Most people would have scheduled a major pity party at that point; but Jacob's faithfulness, combined with his encounter with God, must have changed him. He made a crucial choice that represents a choice *every faithful servant must make* sometime: **He chose to start again.**

When people disappoint us through betrayal, deceit or outright persecution, it is difficult to see them sail along through life in apparent prosperity and blessing while we suffer. It pushes us to the limit to take every thought captive when we would prefer to take someone else captive.

Laban was becoming prosperous because of *Jacob's faithfulness!* To make matters worse, Laban didn't even pay him. Then Laban even cheated him out of his contracted wage and gave him Leah instead of Rachel. Nevertheless, Jacob chose to pick up his servant's towel again and labor for another seven years to win the love of his life. It reminds me of what Jesus said about what I call "the weapon of servanthood":

> But I tell you not to resist an evil person. But whoever slaps you on your right cheek, turn the other to him also. If anyone wants

to sue you and take away your tunic, let him have your cloak also. And whoever compels you to go one mile, go with him two.[13]

We encourage you to start again, no matter how severe your disappointment may be. If you get knocked down and knocked out unjustly by those you serve, *choose to start again in God*. It is the right choice to put you back on the path of joy and success in God's service.

Two of Dave's acquaintances, Roy and Patricia Perkins, established a small mission station in Mozambique several years ago at the height of a civil war raging between the armed forces of the ruling Frelimo faction and the resistance faction called Renamo.[14] There was no hospital for more than 100 miles, and Roy and Patricia were working in dense bush country.

Although their main purpose was to provide primary health care, the Perkinses often took in destitute cases and had to smuggle medical supplies into Mozambique with great difficulty. At night, they often heard gunfire, bomb explosions and even the shouts of soldiers in the distance. On one occasion, soldiers came through and stripped the mission of anything remotely valuable.

Then one night, the Perkinses lay in bed and watched while soldiers literally stole their curtains by pulling them through the window openings after they cut through the mosquito gauze with their bayonets. They managed to escape and, after spending the night in hiding, they returned to their house at first light only to discover that it had been completely ransacked.

Abducted in the Night!

Some months later, the couple heard soldiers come to their station compound again one night. They watched again as their curtains were ripped from their railings through the window. They managed to slip out of the house and hide in the bush. On other such occasions the soldiers had left, but this time the soldiers realized the Perkinses had been there and began to search for them.

The Perkinses had an elderly lady named Joan Goodman with them who, due to the extreme haste of their escape, was wearing only a thin sleeping garment and a pair of slippers. Roy and Patricia and a fourth member of their party, 24-year-old American Kindra Bryan, were in their pajamas; but only one of them had shoes. The soldiers eventually found and abducted them, along with a Zimbabwean couple and their 18-month-old baby, and then destroyed the mission station before leaving.

The terrorists marched their captives through the night and rested out of sight of the soldiers the following day. This pattern went on for 40 days and nights; the slippers began to wear out, and the captives remained in their nightclothes for some time. As the weeks wore on, the captives lost weight at an alarming rate due to the extreme stress and limited food they received.

Even after the 40 days of forced night marches ended, the Renamo rebel terrorists held the Perkins party for several months. Eventually the captives' plight became an international incident when it was learned that one person in the party was a citizen of the United States. After the American government exerted extreme pressure on the Renamo, the abductors agreed to march the captives to the border of Malawi and deliver them to the American chargé d'affaires there.

A Dear Price for Their Service

By the time the Perkinses and their companions finally tasted freedom, their bodies were in poor condition. In the natural, these medical missionaries faced a devastating situation. They had paid a dear price for their service to the needy and the sick in Mozambique, and everything they built through years of labor, sacrifice and service was destroyed.

The United States offered to bring the Perkinses to the United States and grant them refugee status, but they chose to return to Zimbabwe and South Africa in the interim. People often asked them, "What are you going to do now?" Their unhesitating reply was always the same: *"We are going back."*

The circumstances may have changed, but they were convinced that God had not changed His mind. Like Jacob, Roy and Patricia Perkins had every reason to be disappointed in the natural. Some would even question whether or not God was even in it. Nevertheless, *they chose to start serving again,* even in their disappointment.

The Perkinses are servants. They knew the cost of their commitment to return to Mozambique, but they chose to start again anyway. They had a divine mission to fulfill.

No matter what disappointments you have experienced in the past and no matter what you may face in the future, take heart because Jesus has overcome. Start again.

Jacob Started Over and Served with a Good Attitude

Jacob worked another seven years with no wages and God began to prosper him because he had a *good attitude.* Even Laban realized something supernatural was going on. When Jacob completed his second set of seven years and told Laban he was ready to go, Laban said, "Please stay, if I have found favor in your eyes, *for I have learned by experience that the LORD has blessed me for your sake.*"[15]

When Laban asked Jacob to name his wages, Jacob didn't cite a certain salary or promotion request. He said, in essence, "Don't give me anything." Instead, he asked Laban to let him go through the flocks and remove "the speckled and spotted sheep, and all the brown ones among the lambs, and the spotted and speckled among the goats."[16]

Jacob was actually saying, "I will remove all of the mongrels, the ones that are worthless and unwanted, the cast-off animals that pollute the herd. Let me remove the weak and feeble animals from your herds—the very animals you don't want. I'll take the animals that give you a bad name." Jacob had a good attitude in his serving, and God honored it. The Bible says, "Thus the man became exceedingly prosperous, and had large flocks, female and male servants, and camels and donkeys."[17]

Servants of God who serve others with a good attitude despite mistreatment, misunderstanding and wrongs committed against them receive God's visible favor and blessing. This principle is evident in the lives of Joseph, Moses, David, Mordecai (Esther's older cousin and guardian) and Daniel. The most they did in times of adversity was seek the Lord in prayer, and He handled their problems for them. In every case, godly servants must have a good attitude.

PERSEVERE FOR A PURPOSE

The book of Ruth is a journal of God's faithfulness to three faithful people. If you recall the story, Naomi was left with nothing but the company of her two young daughters-in-law after her husband and two sons died in the land of Moab.

Naomi was too old to remarry and bear two more sons in the Hebrew tradition as husbands for Orpah and Ruth. She called in her daughters-in-law and released them from any further obligations, assuming they would seek husbands from their own nation of Moab. Neither of the young widows wanted to leave her, but Orpah finally accepted Naomi's offer and returned to the home of her parents.

Ruth somehow looked beyond the desperate circumstances of the natural to see her true inheritance in the family of her late husband. She realized she had gained more than a husband and a father-in-law, both of whom were gone. She had gained a "mother-in-love" who walked with God. Ruth's relationship with Naomi transcended the dry regulations of the law and entered the limitless realm of love. It was through Naomi's example of faith that Ruth first gained access to the anointing of the God of Abraham, Isaac and Jacob.

Ruth made one of the most dramatic declarations of faith, loyalty and commitment in the Bible:

> Entreat me not to leave you, or to turn back from following after you; for wherever you go, I will go; and wherever you lodge, I will lodge; *your people shall be my people,* and *your God, my God.* Where you die, I will die, and there will I be buried.[18]

Naomi decided to return to Bethlehem, and Ruth went with her. They arrived in Bethlehem with virtually no possessions, so Ruth suggested that she glean grain from barley fields owned by Boaz, a wealthy relative of her late father-in-law. Only the poor or aliens were permitted to glean the grain left behind by the harvest workers,[19] so this shows us Ruth didn't have a problem with false pride. She clearly *looked beyond* the acquisition of grain toward the possibility of winning the favor of Boaz.[20]

Boaz also demonstrated the ability to *look through and beyond the natural* when he visited his barley fields at harvest and picked Ruth out of all of the men and women who worked for him. It is clear through their conversation that Boaz carefully kept track of the welfare of his family members.

They Looked Through and Beyond Their Differences to Find God's Will

Boaz told Ruth to remain in his fields and to follow his handmaidens, or female servants, in the field. He instructed his workers to leave Ruth alone. This leads Ruth to ask:

> *"Why have I found favor in your eyes,* that you should take notice of me, *since I am a foreigner?"* And Boaz answered and said to her, "It has been fully reported to me, all that you have done for your mother-in-law since the death of your husband, and how you have left your father and your mother and the land of your birth, and have come to a people whom you did not know before. The LORD repay your work, and *a full reward be given you by the LORD God of Israel, under whose wings you have come for refuge."* Then she said, "Let me find favor in your sight, my lord; for you have comforted me, and have spoken kindly to your maidservant, *though I am not like one of your maidservants."*[21]

Boaz clearly perceived that Ruth had cast away all of her natural credentials, resources and hopes and had pinned all of her hope on the God of Israel. Something about Ruth's daring faith in God captured his heart. What an amazing story!

Boaz *could have* rushed past his fields and not bothered to ask about one of the many women working the fields or resting in the farm buildings. He could have treated it like any other day, but he was sensitive enough to listen with his eyes and see with his ears. Ruth and Boaz had a divine appointment with destiny that day, and they were sensitive enough to act on the gentle prompting of the Lord by *looking through and beyond the natural.*

I have often driven past the fertile fruit and vegetable fields in the rich agricultural regions of Southern California. The hundreds of farm workers look like tiny dots in the vast expanse of those fields, and I think of them whenever I read this story of Ruth and Boaz.

Boaz Felt God's Nudge to Do What He Had Never Done Before

Boaz was very wealthy, so his fields must have been quite large. He could have seen nothing but little specks as he looked across his field, but he chose to look *through and beyond the obvious and the routine.* He saw the hand of God on a foreign young woman in his fields. He must have sensed the nudge of God to do something he had never done before. He was faithful to investigate the situation of his cousin Naomi after she returned without her husband. Then he was faithful to honor his obligation under Jewish law as Naomi's near-kinsman.[22]

To marry Ruth, he had to buy back all of the land and property of Naomi and her late husband. He would also be responsible to pay any debts that may have remained. Most important of all, Boaz honored his obligation to permit his firstborn son through Ruth to be counted as the son of Ruth's deceased and childless first husband, to carry on his family name. It was a great responsibility and service, but Boaz was faithful.

His obedience produced one of the Bible's great romance stories. After he and Ruth were married, their marriage produced a son named Jesse—the father of David and the early lineage of Jesus Christ.

Ruth is the classic example of someone who learned to persevere for a purpose in the midst of difficulty and disappointment. She was still young when she was suddenly widowed; she had every reason to be disappointed at what life had dealt her. Yet Ruth chose to persevere in one of the most crucial areas in anyone's life, and it signaled a total and permanent change in her life's direction that still affects us to this day.

In Time of Crisis, Ruth Pressed into Her Relationships

Ruth told Naomi, *"Your people shall be my people,* and your God, my God."[23] Ruth obviously understood the importance of relationships. She chose to intertwine her fate with that of her mother-in-law and to put her trust in Jehovah, the God of Israel.

When things are difficult, relationships can either bring comfort or discomfort. When things get tough, that is the time to persevere and draw even closer to the people God puts in your life. Don't evade your trusted relationships; embrace them.

One time Carol and I knew a young woman who lived in the midwest area of the United States; she was like a daughter in the Lord to us.[24] She loved the Lord, but after she graduated from school, she left the area to take a job at an upscale ski resort in Colorado. Although it was a very beautiful place, she became lonely and entered into an immoral relationship with an Iranian Muslim man. The situation eventually became very desperate and her father asked us to go to the resort to meet with her.

To lower the intensity level, we decided to have the conversation with the young woman while walking along a trail in a nearby forest. As we spoke, she began to weep, and the Spirit of the Lord helped us to show her what was really going on in her situation.

Her Relationship to Jesus Was Restored

This young woman chose to run *to* us instead of away from us. She chose to persevere for the restoration of her relationship with Jesus, even in the midst of failure and sin. Before we left, she agreed to work through the situation with her father. This in turn opened the way for her father to rescue her and take her back home to a safe environment.

Throughout this crisis, we chose to love instead of condemn. This young prodigal daughter already knew she was wrong; she just didn't know how to make things right again. Never once did any of us condemn her; we simply loved her in Jesus.

The good news is that this girl moved forward in the Lord. She is very happily married today and she is an excellent mother. When she failed and sinned, she did not run from her godly relationships; she per-severed for a purpose. She wanted to be free and she wanted her rela-tionship with God to be restored.

When you are in a crisis, there are two basic areas in which you should take refuge: your family and your salvation. When you face a dis-appointment or crisis, retreat to your family and to your God. Such retreat is not defeat. Cultivate relationships on Earth and in heaven that will shelter you from life's storms.

Ruth Put All of Her Hope in God

Ruth dealt with her biggest disappointment by choosing to trust the God of Naomi. She chose to stake all of her hopes, dreams and desires for the future on the God of Israel. She wasn't double-minded or timid either. She boldly declared, "Your people shall be my people, and *your God, my God!*"

She persevered in her relationship with her mother-in-law and, through her, discovered the reality of the God of eternity.

During a crisis you can either run to God or you can run away from Him. Some people shake their heads in the middle of a crisis and say, "I

During a crisis, the most dangerous thing we can do is run away and deny God the opportunity to work in our lives.

wonder why God did this to me?" Inevitably they walk away from their rela-tionship with God. Other people run to God when a crisis unexpectedly strikes. They use God as their own "spare wheel" to get their lives back on the road. Once they roll past the crisis, they put away their divine spare tire and promptly forget that God delivered them.

When Carol and I talked with the trou-bled young woman while the three of us walked a forest trail, I asked her, "Do you still love Jesus?" She immediately said, "With all my heart!" Then I asked our young friend, "Is your love for Jesus greater than your love for your sin?" She chose Jesus and never looked back.

We all experience moments in life when we must answer the question, "Do I love Jesus more than I love my sin?" The key to forgiveness and victory rests in the way we answer that very important question. The most dangerous thing we can do is run away and deny God the opportunity to work in our lives. That puts us in a position where God cannot communicate with us. The solution is simple: Face your disappointments by running to God.

Ruth Did Not Cling to Her Natural Security

When crisis strikes, most people naturally cling to what is most familiar to them. That usually includes temporal things like homes, culture, possessions and religion. Ruth refused to cling to those things. She set her sights on a far greater hope. Many modern-day saints had the opportunity to cling to their natural security in times of disappointment, but they chose to run to God. They pursued God and fulfilled their destinies in Christ, enriching the Bride of Christ as well.

As a young girl of 18, Jackie Pullinger left the comforts of her native England and boarded a boat for Hong Kong. She entered the walled city that was filled with opium smugglers, drug dealers and prostitutes. Everything around her was foreign to her culture, but she simply chose to do what God told her to do.

Jackie's decision to obey God's call to Hong Kong produced a major breakthrough in our understanding of spiritual warfare. She learned how to deal with drug addiction and set people free through the power of the Holy Spirit. This only happened after Jackie persevered through a difficult period of five years. Then the supernatural breakthrough came.

Peter Marshall was considered one of America's greatest preachers when he served as chaplain to the United States Senate. People stood in awe of this man's ministry. But he died while still a young man. His wife, Catherine, rose from her grief and despair to become one of the great "mothers" of the modern Church.

It is very possible that many churches would not be in existence today if Catherine Marshall had not risen from her disappointment to accept a divine appointment as one of the leaders and saints who ushered in the mighty move of the Holy Ghost in our day. She could have quit when her husband died. Instead, she chose to persevere and run to God in her time of crisis.

The Easy Way Isn't Always the Right Way

More often than not, the right way seems, at face value, to be the most costly way to go. But in the long term, God's best for us is all that matters.

In April 1999, America was rocked by reports of the Columbine High School massacre in Colorado. The nation was stunned at the cold-blooded murder of 13 students by two of their fellow students. Yet in the midst of the tragedy, there were amazing stories of young Christian students who chose to declare their faith in Jesus Christ as they stared into a gun barrel and faced imminent death.

Those young believers knew their assailants wanted them to deny Jesus. In that moment, it would have been much easier to do that; but they loved Jesus more than their own lives and chose death with Christ rather than life with denial. Millions of viewers around the world watched the funerals for these young martyrs and heard testimony after testimony about their love for the Lord. Many people came to salvation because of their faithfulness in death. *Truly, for these young victims, to live was Christ but to die was gain.*[25]

RESPOND RATHER THAN REACT

Jesus never reacted; He always responded. Imagine the moment when the disciples met Jesus for the first time after His resurrection. The last time they saw Him was the night they all ran out on Him. Mary Magdalene had already announced that she has seen Him, and the disciples were meeting in secret:

> Then, the same day at evening, being the first day of the week, when the doors were shut where the disciples were assembled,

for fear of the Jews, Jesus came and stood in the midst, and said to them, "Peace be with you." When He had said this, He showed them His hands and His side. Then the disciples were glad when they saw the Lord. So Jesus said to them again, "Peace to you! As the Father has sent Me, I also send you." And when He had said this, He breathed on them, and said to them, "Receive the Holy Spirit. If you forgive the sins of any, they are forgiven them; if you retain the sins of any, they are retained."[26]

When the Lord Calls Us to Do More Than Pray

Jesus didn't react in anger or pain; He *responded to the disciples' betrayal and failure with forgiveness.* He had no interest in vengeance; He immediately began to speak to the disciples about forgiveness. He didn't say, "Just look at what you did to Me. Every one of you needs to repent." He simply said, *"Go and forgive other people for their sins."*

Jesus calls us to do more than just have a change of heart. And sometimes He calls us to do more than just pray for a person or situation—He calls our forgiveness into action.

In the garden before Jesus' crucifixion, Peter missed the will of God when he pulled out the sword and lobbed off the ear of Malchus, one of the Lord's captors. Peter had the right weapon but the wrong realm.[27]

Jesus didn't react to Peter's wrong or to Malchus's role in the armed lynch mob. He responded to Peter by telling him to put away his sword. He responded to Malchus with forgiveness and the healing of his ear. Forgiveness always demands a response.

Jesus always responded to anger, failure and wrongdoing with the opposite spirit. When He first saw the disciples after the resurrection, He blessed them and then *He gave* to them as well. He breathed on them and said, "Receive the Holy Spirit,"[28] when He could have said, "Receive the judgment and condemnation you deserve." He also said, "As the Father has sent Me, I also send you,"[29] and gave them the greatest commission of their lives. On the day of Pentecost, the Holy Spirit of God descended on the 120 in the Upper Room in a fiery baptism of power that empowered them for supernatural servanthood.[30] That power to be witnesses is still available to us today and will remain as long as there remain people who have not heard the good news of Christ.

Jesus' Forgiveness Released the Disciples to Their Destiny

The Lord chose to respond to the failure of His heartbroken disciples by serving them, not by condemning them. His forgiveness and faith in them released the disciples to start over again and pursue their divine destiny. The next time Jesus saw the disciples, He blessed and served them by cooking them breakfast.[31]

Our human natures automatically want to react when we are wronged. The God nature in our hearts wants to react with a pure spirit.

One time, Carol and I watched a television report about a woman who had been brutally raped. The assailant was captured and imprisoned, but his victim became convicted that she needed to respond with forgiveness. She and her husband actually visited the rapist in prison and told him they had chosen to forgive him and so had Jesus.

As time went by, the couple led the convicted rapist to Christ and befriended him. Upon his release from prison, the couple took him into their home and helped him reintegrate into society. The ultimate forgiveness shown by that brave couple demonstrates the true power of forgiveness in Jesus Christ. They responded with pure hearts rather than with hearts filled with vengeance.[32]

Servanthood is not always easy, *but it is both a dignity and a delight* if we learn how to tap the power of faithfulness. On any given day we must make right choices whether we experience disappointment or victory. God delights to honor faithfulness in His servant sons and daughters.

CAN YOU STICK LIKE GLUE?

Paul made it clear that God seeks out ordinary people of no reputation or outward credentials just so He can honor them and do great exploits through them for His glory.[33] All it takes for the ordinary to become great in God's kingdom is a servant heart and the ability to stick like glue to His purposes and abiding presence.

If you want to make a fresh start in your service to the Lord, there is no better time to do it than *now*. Pray these words from your heart and trust God to do the work in your heart and life:

Father, I come to You in Jesus' name. By Your grace, I look beyond my deepest disappointments and impossibilities in this moment. Open my eyes and ears to perceive Your kingdom in new ways, so I can serve others in Your wisdom and power.

I acknowledge my failures and weaknesses, but in Jesus' name, I choose to be faithful and true to everything You have asked me to do. My goal isn't to be great but to be faithful to You and those You bring into my life.

Be glorified in me, Lord. Thank You for giving me a new start today. Please accept my life as a freely given gift, and teach me how to serve with dignity and delight for the rest of my life. In Jesus' holy name I pray, amen.

Notes
1. Matthew 25:21.
2. Gene Edwards, *Our Mission* (Auburn, ME: Christian Books, 1984), pp. 65-67. Used by permission.
3. Proverbs 27:17.
4. Acts 1:21,22.
5. See 2 Corinthians 12:9.
6. John 16:33.
7. 1 Corinthians 4:2.
8. Nehemiah 8:10.
9. See Genesis 27:41—28:4.
10. See Genesis 28:10-22.
11. See Genesis 29:1-18.
12. See Genesis 29:20-28.
13. Matthew 5:39-41.

14. "Frelimo" is an acronym for "Frente de Libertacao de Mocambique." Frelimo origi-
    nally was a movement for independence from Portugal. After Mozambique estab-
    lished its independence, Frelimo leaders ruled the country and leaned more and
    more toward Socialism and Marxism. This turn worried certain officials in the
    United States and some of Mozambique's neighboring countries (including the
    Republic of South Africa during the apartheid era). They began to offer financial
    and military training assistance to the Renamo ("Resistencia National
    Mocambicana"), a group seeking to destabilize the economy and social structure of
    Mozambique through terrorism, so they could overthrow the Frelimo leadership.
    Unfortunately, both sides committed unspeakable atrocities in the name of their
    respective causes. The story of Roy and Patricia Perkins and their party is even more
    miraculous in light of the violence of the Mozambique conflict.
15. Genesis 30:27, italics mine.
16. Genesis 30:32.
17. Genesis 30:43.
18. Ruth 1:16,17, italics mine.
19. See Leviticus 19:9,10; 23:22; Deuteronomy 24:19-21.
20. See Ruth 2:1,2.
21. Ruth 2:10-13, italics mine.
22. See Ruth 4:1-17.
23. Ruth 1:16.
24. The details of this story have been changed to protect the people involved.
25. See Philippians 1:21. For an insightful understanding of what occurred at
    Columbine and how Christians should respond, read Bruce Porter's book *The
    Martyr's Torch* (Shippensburg, PA: Destiny Image Publishers, Fresh Bread
    Publishing, 1999).
26. John 20:19-23.
27. See Luke 22:49-51; John 18:10,11.
28. John 20:22. Please note that Jesus imparted the abiding presence of the Holy Spirit
    to the disciples on this occasion. In Luke 24:49, Jesus said, "Behold, I send the
    Promise of My Father upon you; but tarry in the city of Jerusalem *until you are endued
    with power from on high*" (italics mine) just before He ascended to the Father in the
    transfiguration. This promise was fulfilled in the Upper Room in Acts 2 when the
    120 (and many thereafter) received the baptism of the Holy Spirit and were endued
    with power *to be witnesses*.
29. John 20:21.
30. See Acts 1:8; 2:1-11.
31. See John 21:9-13.
32. We are not proposing a new doctrine in which victims of rape or other violent
    crimes must take in their attackers and help reintegrate them into society. I share
    this true story to illustrate an unusual demonstration of God's grace. We are simply
    required—and empowered—by God to forgive (for *our* well-being as much as for
    those who have wronged us).
33. See this amazing passage in 1 Corinthians 1:26-31.

CHAPTER TEN

SERVING WITH THE PREPARATION OF ANTICIPATION

Good servants worthy of a "well done" serve the Lord in the same way that skilled waiters in fine restaurants serve their customers. There is no thumb twiddling—only a great deal of *anticipation.*

People who dine at fine restaurants in New York or Paris often experience a measure of disappointment when they return to their favorite restaurants at home. What is the difference? Sometimes it's the food, but most often people say they miss the *service* they experienced in the nicer restaurants. Many restaurants are capable of preparing five-star cuisine, but few of them seem to understand how to provide five-star service. The difference between the waiters who "have it" and those who don't is their attitude and approach toward *serving.*

The great waiters take personal pride in their ability to *anticipate* every need of their customers *in advance.* The moment you finish your soup course, the waiter is beside you *waiting* to remove the unneeded dishes and dinnerware. Your beverage glass or cup rarely reaches the two-thirds-filled state before your waiter is there with more—and you never have to ask.

Politeness is mandatory, even when dealing with difficult customers who are barely understandable. The universal mark of excellence among waiters is the statement by their customers that they made them feel like royalty.

THE ANTICIPATION FACTOR SEPARATES GOOD SERVICE FROM EXTRAORDINARY SERVICE

People who enjoy the fine cuisine offered in such restaurants maintain that the waiting skills of the less-than-best waiter appear to lack that vital *anticipation factor* that separates good service from extraordinary service.

Perhaps that vital anticipation factor is missing from our understanding of biblical servanthood as well. Christians too often equate waiting on the Lord with sitting and doing nothing. I have never found that job description anywhere in God's Word.

On the contrary, Jesus commanded us to *occupy*, or "do business," until He comes.[1] Paul said, "Through love serve one another."[2]

We wait on the Lord through worship—whether private or public—anticipating heavenly desire. We also wait on the Lord by waiting on His customers. You fulfill the desires of the Boss by taking care of His customers as if He were there with you. It was Jesus who said, "Assuredly, I say to you, inasmuch as you did it to one of the least of these My brethren, you did it to Me."[3] The Lord's "brethren" include the hungry, the thirsty, the homeless, the naked, the sick and the imprisoned. Few of us are prepared to anticipate *their* needs, yet that is what the Boss expects us to do.

D A V I D   S P E A K S

The anticipation factor Tommy mentioned is a rare but highly valued commodity in the Church today. I have been blessed to minister with a number of exceptional servants over the years I have carried the cross and bowl.

One of these servants accompanied me to the island nation of Haiti just about the time it was invaded by the United States and the United Nations several years ago. My close friend from Cape Town, Rod Palmer, demonstrated the true heart of a servant throughout the length of our stay.

We had to struggle through a number of airports during our journey to Haiti from South Africa, and the heaviest and most difficult item we dragged along with us was my equipment trunk. It contained my wooden cross and bowl, the water-tank contraption, a large supply of towels, a camping stool, rubber shoes and enough extra items to make the sturdiest elephant groan at the thought of the load.

I Came to Serve You

On this particular trip, in addition to my trunk, I also had a large suitcase and Roddy had his own load of gear. During one of the most difficult moments, Roddy suddenly grabbed the trunk with all my gear and hoisted it onto his shoulders. I protested and noted that he was already heavily loaded down with his own baggage. Roddy just said, "No, *I came to serve you.*" No matter how much I complained or protested, he simply would not let me do a thing.

Roddy continued to anticipate even the smallest of needs and opportunities to serve throughout the trip. Once we arrived in Haiti, we had to stay in a room that would definitely *not* make any "best hotels of the world" list. Aside from the extremely cramped quarters, the place didn't have a proper bathroom in any sense of the term. It had a toilet, but there was no gas trap in the drainpipe, which is something most people in modern nations expect automatically (in other words, the toilet smelled terribly *all the time* since the plumbing system imported exotic smells into our room directly from the sewer system).

Nothing in the bathroom would work, although there was a form of running water dribbling from the shower. Each morning when I came out of the shower, Roddy did the one thing he could do to make the place a bit nicer—he faithfully made up my bed. It was a small service that carried a large message to me.

Sometimes I would mention to Roddy that we needed to do a particular task the next day or that I needed to contact a particular person. He knew that I was really asking for a friendly reminder about those items, but Roddy is a servant. The next day without fail, as I prepared to contact the person I'd mentioned, Rod would tell me he had already done it. He was an amazing anticipator who always managed to stay one jump ahead in everything I wanted to do. He simply wanted to serve because he is a true servant.

The Big "A" Word

True servants like Roddy always anticipate the needs and expectations of those they serve. Joseph, the youngest son of Jacob and Rachel, rose from the position of house slave to the second most powerful position in Egypt under Pharaoh. He was intimately familiar with the big *A* word of servanthood.

Joseph listened to the voice of God and *anticipated* the coming famine in Egypt. He prepared the Egyptian nation for the coming drought through an ingenious system of localized storage sites and mandatory grain rationing during seven years of abundant harvest. When the seven years of drought began, Egypt alone among the countries in that region was ready with plenty of reserve grain.

Joseph the servant became a blessing and lifesaver for Pharaoh and all of Egypt because he did not wait for the famine to strike. He anticipated the need and prepared for it in advance.

He also realized that God was the mover and motivator behind his career and calling as a servant. Joseph, the one who chose to start over and serve under another with a good attitude, told the brothers who had betrayed him:

> I am Joseph your brother, whom you sold into Egypt. But now, do not therefore be grieved or angry with yourselves because you sold me here; *for God sent me before you to preserve life.* . . . God sent me before you to *preserve a posterity for you* in the earth, and *to save your lives* by a great deliverance. So now *it was not you who sent me here, but God;* and He has made me a father to Pharaoh, and lord of all his house, and a ruler throughout all the land of Egypt.[4]

Joseph was a true servant, but many who claim to be servants are not. Anyone who always has to be told what to do is *not* a servant. I encourage people to give themselves the servant test by asking the question: Do I always have to be told what to do by those I serve? If the answer is yes, then something needs to change.

MOTHERS TEND TO BE NATURAL ANTICIPATORS

The ability to anticipate includes the strategic ability to *think ahead*. I've noticed that mothers tend to be natural anticipators out of necessity.

Whether the family is making a quick shopping trip or packing for a weeklong camping adventure, it is the mom who thinks ahead and packs even the most obscure pieces of equipment, utensils, first-aid items or favorite toys.

In the commercial world, corporations and manufacturers seek out the most skilled prognosticators, or forecasters of future trends and needs, so their companies can be prepared ahead of time for anticipated growth, challenges or customer demand. Servants need to think ahead, whether they serve in the church, in the mission field, in an office building or on the manufacturing-plant floor.

Some of the greatest servants in local churches around the world are those brave individuals who operate the sound systems in service after service. These servants of God usually arrive long before any scheduled meeting or service to set up equipment, put the microphones in place and run out microphone cables. Most of them also spend additional hours laboriously maintaining the sound equipment when no one else is around.

THE SERVANT AT THE SOUNDBOARD

Maintaining the sound equipment is generally the easiest part of the job of running a sound system. It is the faithful sound person who incurs the combined wrath of exasperated worship team members, the frustrated pastor, fuming singers and special guests, and the best angry stares the congregation can muster! What do these people do to deserve such concentrated anger and public disapproval? It usually comes down to a rapidly developing technical problem that creates an ear-splitting squeal in the sound system or to a problem created by a sound person who has failed to *anticipate* a need on the platform.

I am obviously making a generalization, but in a sense, the sound person can almost hold the anointing captive with the sound controls at his or her fingertips. Two things are at risk: the ever-fleeting attention span of the people in the congregation or audience, and the presence of the Holy Spirit who can be grieved by our insensitivity or ineptness.

Time and again, I've watched ministers move toward a microphone with a word from the Lord at sensitive points in a worship service only to discover the volume on the microphone hasn't been turned on. It finally comes to life after the minister has pantomimed the first three or four sentences, but by then the anointing has already begun to lift because the congregation is doing its best to pin the sound person to the wall with their best steely stares.

This happens most often to sound technicians who react only after a problem arises instead of *anticipating* the need to raise the volume of a microphone when the lead minister steps toward a microphone. I can tell you this: It is a positive joy to work with a competent sound person who anticipates every need and is spiritually sensitive to the flow of the Holy Spirit in a meeting! I pray for God's blessing on every sound person in the Kingdom. Sound persons—and every servant of God—absolutely flourish in their service once they etch the *A* word into their spirits.

A Wonderfully Gifted Spiritual Anticipator

Gerry Armstrong is a dear friend who lives in London, England. He is a wonderfully gifted spiritual anticipator who served our ministry in a unique way. For many years I wore an imported walking shoe to help my feet survive the thousands of miles I walk each year in the course of my ministry.

These extremely comfortable and well-made shoes had leather uppers that remained dry and soft, even when they got wet. They exhibited a technology that was years ahead of its time (the modern-day sneaker or running shoe has just now caught up with this shoe). These shoes were not available in South Africa, so my dear friend Gerry made it his personal task to keep me well supplied with them.

Somehow Gerry made sure that a new pair of shoes was *waiting for me before the pair I was wearing had worn out*. His careful anticipation of my needs proved invaluable during a particularly difficult ministry tour on foot. I developed an infection in one foot when I was out on the road, and the foot swelled up like an out-of-shape football. Finally I could no longer walk and had to receive medical attention.

After I recovered, it was very difficult to return to the rigors of the road. Once again, Gerry had a brand-new set of those comfortable imported shoes waiting for me, and his thoughtful gift made my return to "the foot ministry" much easier than it would have been otherwise. I am grateful for genuine servants of God like Gerry who are so faithful to think ahead and anticipate the needs of those they serve in the Body of Christ and in the world.

HOW A SERVANT DEALS WITH THE UNEXPECTED

It is the preparation of anticipation that helps true servants deal with the unexpected. Imagine how David, the young shepherd boy, felt during those times he confronted a lion or a bear attacking his father's sheep. He was prepared in the Spirit because he knew his God. David told King Saul that he grabbed each lion by the beard and killed it, and he gave God the glory for the deed.[5] This is the way a servant deals with the unexpected.

If there was a beatitude of servanthood, perhaps it would read: Blessed are the flexible, for they shall bend and not be broken.

Jesus constantly dealt with the unexpected in His earthly ministry. In my mind, one of the most unexpected challenges He faced occurred the day some scribes and Pharisees came to Him in the Temple and threw down a woman caught in the act of adultery.

Jesus was surrounded by a self-righteous mob of men with rocks in their hands, and they were ready to stone the woman to death. I'm sure Jesus knew that if the stones were not for her, then they were probably meant for Him. He began to serve the woman by humbling her assailants and forgiving her sins. Jesus chose the right weapon for the right realm.[6]

I hope your unexpected challenge doesn't have the drama and danger of a confrontation with a lion or an angry rock-wielding mob. Even if it is simply the need to adapt cheerfully to an unexpected change of plans at the last moment, you must anticipate and be prepared for the unexpected. If there was a beatitude of servanthood, perhaps it would read, *Blessed are the flexible, for they shall bend and not be broken.*

THE IMPORTANCE OF PREPARATION

Jesus was a master servant who understood the importance of preparation. When His mother told him there was no more wine at the wedding in Cana, the first thing Jesus did was command the servants to *prepare* the water pots.[7] Only then did He turn the water into wine for the wedding guests. He also told His disciples to *prepare* the crowd of 5,000 men before He miraculously fed them.[8] Another time, Jesus sent His disciples ahead to *prepare* for Him before He mounted a young donkey and entered Jerusalem.[9]

Sometimes the preparations of the Lord were incredibly detailed and prophetic in nature, even when they concerned natural needs:

And He sent Peter and John, saying, "Go and *prepare* the Passover for us, that we may eat." So they said to Him, "Where do You want us to prepare?" And He said to them, "Behold, when you have entered the city, a man will meet you carrying a pitcher of water; follow him into the house which he enters. Then you shall say to the master of the house, 'The Teacher says to you, "Where is the guest room where I may eat the Passover with My disciples?"' Then he will show you a large, furnished upper room; there make ready."[10]

True servants also anticipate needs by being *spiritually sensitive ahead of time.* Some years ago while I was making my initial transcontinental ministry walk through South Africa, a friend named Ron Watermeyer sensed in the Spirit that I needed his assistance. He immediately took a leave from his job and traveled with his wife and their small children many hundreds of miles to meet Carol and me (and our children) on the road.

WE WEREN'T THE ONLY THINGS WORN OUT

At that time, we were growing weary because of the exceptional pace of the ministry both on and off the road. We weren't the only things that were worn out. Our car and trailer were in serious need of repair as well.

Ron had two purposes in mind when he arrived—he was determined to see that all of our vehicles were repaired and made fully roadworthy; and he wanted to make sure Carol and me were refreshed body, soul and spirit.

While another dear friend hosted Carol and me with our children at a small holiday hotel, Ron took our vehicles to the large city of Durban to have them repaired. During that time, our entire family was truly blessed, refreshed and restored physically and spiritually.

Ron returned with fully repaired and reconditioned vehicles, and a week later we took to the road again feeling blessed by his supernatural servanthood. Ron was spiritually sensitive to the prompting of the Holy Spirit, and he walked in the true servanthood anointing of God.

Servanthood by definition includes virtually every form of ministry, but the importance of being spiritually sensitive ahead of time is especially crucial in the area of public ministry in the Word of God and personal ministry in prayer.

Just before Roddy and I left for the Haiti trip I mentioned earlier, the Holy Spirit warned us during a time of spiritual warfare in prayer that we would encounter demonic resistance in that nation. Forewarned by the Lord, we entered Haiti armed with the preparation of anticipation.

It is said that some 300 years ago, the leaders of Haiti dedicated their nation to Satan in a pact to win freedom from a colonial power. At the very least, Haiti enjoys the notorious distinction of being a modern-day haven for voodoo practices and witchcraft.

One night, Rod and I were ministering to about 400 people just outside the Haitian capital of Port-au-Prince when I felt prompted to pray for those seeking the baptism of the Holy Spirit, which is described in the book of Acts. This was a routine ministry function I had facilitated many times before, and usually it is a fairly dignified process: When I begin to pray for people, the Holy Spirit descends on them and some begin to be filled while others just stand quietly. On this night, at least half the crowd came forward to receive the baptism of the Holy Spirit.

EVERY DEMON IN HELL SEEMED TO SHOW UP

We began to pray for the people as usual, but this time it seemed like every demon in hell showed up. People began to scream and others were convulsing. Some of them actually foamed at the mouth and others tried to strangle each other or break up the furniture in the place. It was truly *pandemonium!*[11]

I jumped onto a bench and firmly rebuked the spirits in the crowd in the name of Jesus, and they immediately calmed down. Supernatural servanthood is seldom straightforward, and we must be alert for the unexpected. Roddy and I were not shocked by this unexpected situation because we *anticipated* the potential resistance and *prepared* in advance in prayer. We simply used the authority God has given every believer to command the demons to bow before the name of Jesus Christ.

Spiritually sensitive anticipation plays a crucial role in another area of servanthood most often provided by local churches, although certain individuals serve this way as well. I'm referring to efforts of local churches to help ministers of the gospel "pull aside" for vital times of rest, relaxation and solitude with the Lord.

Even Jesus pulled away for times of prayer and intimate communication with His Father in heaven, but many ministers today rarely take time to be refreshed. I've noticed in my travels that some churches are spiritually sensitive to this need in ministers' lives and other churches are not.

The Church That Always Refreshes Us

Occasionally, Carol and I have the privilege of ministering at a church in the village of Sedgefield, situated along South Africa's famed Garden Route, one of the most beautiful stretches of scenery in that region of the world. When we go to Sedgefield, the church always arranges for us to have a break for a few days after we minister. They put us in a beautiful time-share resort featuring exquisite chalets perched over the edge of the steep dunes several hundred feet above the waves of the sea below. The church graciously stocks the pantry ahead of time and ensures that there are all kinds of fruit and pies in the refrigerator.

Another time, a creative church in Cape Town, South Africa, told us to set aside two extra days on our calendar when we came to minister to their congregation. The church wanted to treat us to a first-class train excursion instead of the usual flight home. We were amused and not really sure what to expect.

After a wonderful time of ministry, we boarded the luxury train and began to relax as it wound its way through the exquisite Hex River Valley. That night we dined sumptuously in an upscale formal dining car—a treat we enjoyed again at breakfast the next morning. We arrived home totally refreshed and exceedingly blessed. This church was *sensitive ahead of time;* its members anticipated our needs and served us in a unique way we will never forget.

Servants of God must always be sensitive to the Holy Spirit when they serve. This is especially important for those who preach the Word or lead the flock of God in some capacity. Sensitivity to the Spirit can make the difference between a powerful, life-changing visitation of God that launches revival, and a brief taste of what could have been if only . . . We can't afford to be insensitive and inflexible to the Spirit of God when He prompts us to do something we've never done before.

Jesus was the ultimate anticipating servant. He spent His entire life on Earth in only two modes—*evangelism*, declaring that the kingdom of heaven was at hand, and *serving*. Everything He did fits in one of these two categories of ministry. *As He served,* He continuously *anticipated* that His Father's kingdom would come and His will would be done on Earth. Now He has transferred His twofold ministry *to us.*

Notes
1. See Luke 19:13, in the context of the kingdom of God.
2. Galatians 5:13.
3. Matthew 25:40.
4. Genesis 45:4-8, italics mine.
5. See 1 Samuel 17:34-37.
6. See John 8:2-11.
7. See John 2:7.
8. See Mark 6:39-44.
9. See Matthew 21:1-10.
10. Luke 22: 8-12, italics mine.
11. I am speaking literally. "Pandemonium" is the name Milton gave to the capital of hell in *Paradise Lost.* It is a compound Greek word meaning "all demons."

CHAPTER ELEVEN

PLUGGING THE LEAKS AND SERVING FOR A LIFETIME

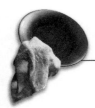

"Anointing leaks; so do Christians."

For several years, Dave has used this unforgettable saying to launch the final session of his Celebration of Servanthood seminars. This phrase reminds me of a story my father, T. F. Tenney, shared with me about something he witnessed during a church service. He saw a young man at the altar praying with what appeared to be uncommon passion, *"Lord, fill me! Lord, fill me!"*

That sounded commendable, but something else my dad heard caused him to think that this particular young man was a person who "got filled" every time there was a revival but who "never lived up to his filling." When I asked why, my dad said he heard an elderly lady across from the young man praying, *"Don't do it, Lord. He leaks!"*

Perhaps the dear sister was really praying, "Lord, repair the leaks before You fill him." The point is that many of us come to church and get all filled up with the glory, power and purity of God. Yet somehow on our way out of God's kitchen, we manage to spill the glass of glory.

The symptoms of heart disease in the Church are alarming: We are too winded and weak in spirit to follow the Great Physician into the streets and participate in His glory.

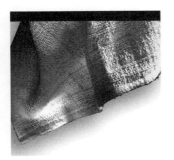

We leak God's heavenly deposit so often and so thoroughly that we get used to maintaining our lives on heavenly fumes instead of on godly fire. Our good intentions are like a shiny but leaky gasoline container: We have the bright red paint signaling our passion, the Christian sticker warning of the combustible power we contain and the capacity markings declaring our wonderful potential to move the world with what is inside us. Yet anyone who actually tries to tap the fuel within us quickly discovers that we really contain mostly volatile fumes and empty promises—all of our real potential leaked out long ago.

GOOD INTENTIONS WITH NO CORRESPONDING ACTION

This is a picture of what happens to us when we accept a life filled with good intentions and no corresponding actions. It is the fatal heart condition of the Church about which James warned us when he said, "Faith without works is dead."[1] The Great Physician is putting His Body on notice: *The stress test is coming.*

The symptoms of heart disease in the Church are alarming: He has found that *we know* more than what *we do*. Our knowledge has exceeded our actions (and His expectations). The pharisaical system ultimately died from complications of these symptoms. We live beneath His promises and below His calling, and we are too winded and weak in spirit to follow Him into the streets and participate in His glory.

Servanthood is exactly what the Doctor has ordered for His overweight, bloated and lethargic Body. It is time to peel ourselves off of the couch of indulgence and lay down our "bless me" milk shakes. There is work to do and excess weight to "lay aside."[2] The Church of inspiration must become the Church of perspiration if we hope to keep up with the Chief Servant and pioneer of our faith.

The cuisine at the Lord's Table is wonderful and exciting, but first somebody has to wash the debris from the soiled feet of sinners and saints alike before they can come to the table. If we won't do it, will the King of glory have to shame us publicly by stooping down to take up once more our fallen towels Himself?

DAVID SPEAKS

Anointing leaks; so do Christians. As one leaky vessel to another, I assure you that I must constantly remind myself about the vision and goals God gave me in the beginning. Most pastors around the world spend much of their lives trying to keep their churches focused on the founding vision God placed in their hearts. We are too easily distracted and too likely to forget the most important things because of all the *other* things.

During the time that Celebration of Servanthood was birthed in my heart after 12 days of prayer and fasting, the Lord began to speak to me about servanthood. I studied the lives of great servants in the Bible and received some very important principles. However, I couldn't get that "leaking" problem out of my mind. I wanted to know how these truths could be made memorable for people like me whose memories take occasional unscheduled holidays.

When I asked the Lord for leakproof wisdom, I sensed He was nudging me with the Scripture passage that says, *"Be still,* and know that I am God; I will be exalted among the nations, I will be exalted in the earth!"[3] That is difficult for a preacher, but I sat at the table with my pen and pad and said, "All right, God. I will not speak until you speak to me."

FOUR HOURS LATER

I sat there with my pad and pen without saying a word for hours. In fact, *four* hours later, nothing had happened. In all that time, I had only written one thing on my pad—the word "servant." It didn't seem particularly profound to me; after all, the Lord and I had been talking and focusing on servants for the past 10 days.

"Is there nothing else?" I asked in prayer. Then I felt the quiet unction of the Holy Spirit say, "That is what I want to say to you." As I stared at this solitary word on my pad, I noticed that the word "servant" had seven letters in it. I felt the Lord say, "That is the key that I want to give you."

There is one letter in "servant" for each day of the week, and that is the key to what we call *everyday servanthood.* The Lord gave me seven keys based on each letter of the word "servant." These keys help us live as servants each day of the week.

Many Christians genuinely want to serve Jesus Christ. They have servant hearts, but they really don't know how to serve. The first step for most of us begins by choosing one individual or couple to serve in Christ's name (any more than one person or one couple can become a distraction). This is not "shotgun servanthood" but one-on-one service from you to another. Once that decision is made, I've found that this simple and practical seven-day pattern has made the difference for thousands of people around the world.

SEVEN KEYS TO EVERYDAY SERVANTHOOD

Day 1: The Letter S in "Servant"

The letter *s* in "servant" stands for the way true servants *speak love* to all they meet and in every situation. If you would be a servant, start the first day of the week by serving others and speak love into their lives. We all need encouragement, love and positive self-worth, but it is amazing to see how many people struggle with and suffer from low self-esteem.

Encouragement costs nothing, and it is a vital need for everyone. So why do we so seldom encourage one another? Select *the person* you are going to serve this week, contact him or her and begin to speak words of love and encouragement into that life. The change that comes to that person's countenance will amaze you.

Never assume that someone doesn't need your words of love and encouragement. *Everyone* needs it: parents, children, bosses (whether they are friendly or hostile), friends, family members and even pastors and ministers (none of us are as perfect as we may appear).

Many people never include their pastor on their "love and encouragement" list because they think, *The pastor walks so closely with the Lord; why would he need encouragement?* Pastors face tremendous pressures every day, and unlike most day jobs, the work of a pastor never seems to end. They quickly learn to live on call—around the clock, seven days a week, all year round.

Many pastors feel they have as many bosses as they do congregation members—and these bosses all seem to have different ideas about the ways things should be done! Can you imagine how weary his shoulders must be, carrying the combined opinions, pressures, urgent needs and disagreements of 50 to several thousand people? Be sensitive, and be quick to speak words of love and encouragement to your pastor.

Never Underestimate the Power of Encouraging Words

It has been my personal observation that ladies seem to struggle with self-esteem more than men do. For some reason, men are more likely to shrug off their concerns about self-esteem and just keep going. Yet time and again I've seen Satan harass godly women with fears and second thoughts about their worth, their performance and their appearance before others. Perhaps it is because women seem to be more sensitive to personal issues than men are. Never underestimate the power of your words of love and encouragement to transform a lady's view of herself and raise her self-esteem.

Carol and I know a young woman whom we love deeply and consider to be our "daughter in the Lord." Her father once told me that when she was in her early teens, she was gangly and she had long straggly hair, protruding teeth and thick glasses. None of that mattered to him, of course. He used to put her on his lap, hug her and say, "You're the most beautiful daughter in the world. You are going to grow into the most stunning woman."

This father *spoke love* to his daughter every single day, and as he spoke love, she began to bloom like a rose. Today, she is a beautiful lady by any measure or definition. She stands out in any crowd as an exceptional lady who is refined and radiates both an inner and outer beauty. She is a mother of refined stature with lovely children and an outstanding husband. She is known for her gracious, encouraging and loving ways.

This beautiful young woman overcame her obstacles because someone bothered to speak love to her. On Day 1, speak love to the person you've chosen to serve. Don't get distracted and try to speak love to the whole church or your entire town. Focus on *the one* God points out and begin to *speak love*.

Day 2: The Letter *E* in "Servant"

The letter *e* in "servant" stands for the ***effective*** way true servants plan, prepare and facilitate serving others. Jesus served His disciples in very effective ways. In one instance after His resurrection, Peter and six other disciples decided to go fishing on the Sea of Tiberias.[4] It seems clear to me that they were despondent over their uncertain future without the physical presence of Jesus in the days to come.

When He called out to them from the shore, the seven men had fished all night without catching anything, even though several of the men were commercial fishermen by trade and training. Jesus chose to bless them at what may have been their lowest moment in several days. It becomes clear that the Master *had effectively prepared and planned* His service to those He loved:

> Then Jesus said to them, "Children, have you any food?" They answered Him, "No." And He said to them, "Cast the net on the right side of the boat, and you will find some." So they cast, and now they were not able to draw it in because of the multitude of fish.
>
> Then, as soon as they had come to land, *they saw a fire of coals there*, and *fish laid on it*, and *bread*. Jesus said to them, "Bring some of the fish which you have just caught."
>
> *"Come and eat breakfast."*[5]

Jesus didn't say, "Well, guys, I think I will bless you now. Have you caught any fish? Let's go and find some wood." The fire was already going, the bread had been baked, and the fish were on the coals and ready to eat. The Master Servant effectively planned His service before He served.

The Good Samaritan Was an Effective Planner

The good Samaritan, whom Jesus described to His disciples, exhibited effective preparation and planning skills in addition to his openhearted acts of mercy. First of all, he was a well-equipped traveler because he had everything he needed to administer first aid to the Jewish victim he found by the side of the road: he had material for bandages, oil and wine (an astringent).[6]

After he loaded the man onto his first-century vehicle, he took him to a nearby inn and cared for him through the night. Then he executed an elaborate plan to provide ongoing, long-term care for the Jewish stranger at his own expense: "On the next day, when he departed, he took out two denarii, gave them to the innkeeper, and said to him, 'Take care of him; and whatever more you spend, when I come again, I will repay you.'"[7]

It is important that we *effectively prepare and plan* our service to others. Some things take a lot of preparation and can be difficult to plan, but the difficulty will be nothing compared to the blessing it releases in your life and the lives of those you serve.

Dee is a pastor's wife who lives in Cape Town, South Africa. This dear friend of ours received a visit from a Swiss girl in their church who was expecting a baby. Dee asked if her friends and family in Switzerland were going to give her a baby shower, and she said, "What's a baby shower?"

Dee Invited the Young Woman to Go Along

Dee explained that it was a party at which friends and relatives of the mother-to-be "shower" her with baby clothing, rattles, comforters and other baby items to bless her. "Oh, we don't have anything like that in Switzerland," the young lady said. Dee quickly replied, "Don't worry, we're going to a baby shower in two days' time" and invited the young woman to go along with her.

Two days later, when they arrived at the baby shower, Dee's young guest discovered to her delight that Dee had organized the baby shower just for her! She had contacted all the ladies in the church, and they worked together to bless the young woman with many gifts and a creative party. That event was neither instant nor easy—it happened because of *effective planning and preparation.*

Sometimes the only things we have to give to the Lord and to others are the sweat of our brow and our ability to plan, prepare and organize. This was the case for a couple we met while they hosted a small pastors' conference in a little coastal village in South Africa. This couple served us and the pastors and their spouses throughout our entire stay, and *this couple was exceptional.* If we were eating cake or something else during a break in the meeting, they would take our plates as soon as we were done. If we reached out a hand for another refreshment, they placed filled glasses in our hands before we could make a request. This couple served us with unbelievable efficiency and diligence. I learned later that they were going through some difficult financial challenges, but they wanted to bless and serve us.

We Combined Our Resources to Bless Them

The next day I spoke to all the pastors and their wives, and we decided to bless them with a retreat of their own to help alleviate the stress they had been experiencing. We combined our resources to send them to the oceanside resort city of Port Elizabeth, where we live, and put them up in a nice beachfront hotel.

Everyone chipped in extra money, so the couple could dine at a top-notch restaurant each night; and we made sure they had transportation while they were there. Just before they arrived, Carol placed some beautiful flowers, gifts and a card in their room.

That couple ministered to those at the conference with everything they had to give. We were all very blessed by the couple's selfless service, and we realized we could not alleviate their long-term financial situation; but we decided to bless them with everything we had to give. Once again, our service had to be *effectively prepared and planned.*

(That couple so enjoyed serving us and the guest ministers and their spouses at our small conference that they felt led to start a catering business. It has provided them with a good living, and they still operate the business at this writing—catering food for many hundreds of people at conferences each month. God delights to show Himself faithful to faithful servants.)

Day 3: The Letter *R* in "Servant"

The letter *r* in "servant" stands for the responsibility of God's servants to *reveal Jesus.* On the first day of the week, you spoke love. The second day you effectively prepared and planned. On the third day—the day of new life—*reveal Jesus.*

Find a suitable Scripture to share with the person you've been serving, even if the person does not know the Lord. Then say, "You know, this morning as I was spending time with God, I felt that He wanted me to tell you this." Then read or quote the Scripture verse the Lord has given you. Finally, you can reveal Jesus by telling them an interesting story or testimony about the goodness of God and how you have personally seen Him in action.

I remember a young surfer with long hair, wearing an earring, baggy shorts and sandals. He became convicted during a Celebration of Servanthood conference. He decided that he wanted to serve, but he wanted to serve at the point of his need by doing something he normally wouldn't do. Since he especially disliked going shopping with his mother (he was a teenage boy, and it just wasn't the cool thing to do), he knew what he had to do.

When the moment of truth arrived, he discovered he was going shopping in the company of both his mother *and* his grandmother. He faithfully followed behind in his best surfer outfit and pushed their cart or carried their parcels as needed.

On the way home the three shoppers decided to stop at the hospital to visit his grandfather, who was very ill. As the young man sat with his mother and grandmother around his grandfather's bed, he suddenly asked, "Could I have some moments alone with Granddad?" When everyone else left the room, he began to share the gospel with his grandfather and led him to Jesus.

He Chose to Serve and Revealed Jesus to His Grandfather

When the mother and grandmother returned to the ward, the young surfer went for a walk in the hospital garden. He was still in the garden when they came and told him his grandfather had passed away. This young man obediently *chose to serve* by going shopping and was able to *reveal Jesus* to his grandfather and lead him to the Lord just moments before he died. The Scriptures declare that "the testimony of Jesus is the spirit of prophecy."[8]

If you share testimonies and stories about the Lord's faithfulness in your life with someone who doesn't believe in the Lord, don't be surprised if they *join in!* They often respond by saying something like, "Yes, God also did such-and-such for me, and He did thus-and-so for my aunt Edna." A spirit of thanksgiving seems to come over them although they don't even know the Lord!

In such instances I love to share about the overflow of God's provision for us. My family lives in incredible blessing because, by the very nature of our ministry, every day seems to produce miraculous stories of God's provision. Today our ministry is relatively well known in South Africa and is emerging in the United States, but in the early days it was a real faith walk. At times, Carol and the children would go ahead to the next city or town while I continued walking along the road with my cross and bowl. They would check into a trailer park even though we didn't have enough money to pay for staying there on the following morning. Occasionally, a motorist would stop to greet me on the road and give me the money we needed to pay for the trailer park once I reunited with my family that night. *That is simply the overwhelming goodness of God.* I am convinced that God *gives all of us* miracles in our lives so that we can *reveal Jesus* to other people. These miracles have the power to capture attention, touch hearts and stir up faith in God.

Day 4: The Letter *V* in "Servant"

The letter *v* in "servant" stands for the need to **verify** things with the person you will serve. On the simplest level, I never grab a person's feet and slam them into my foot-washing bowl. I ask them if they would allow me the privilege of washing their feet beforehand. If you feel the Lord wants you to bless a lady with "the works" at the hairdresser's, you need to *verify* some details by saying "I would like to bless you tomorrow with a hairdo. Is tomorrow okay?" If you plan to take a single mother's or a widow's car to the garage for repairs or bless a couple with a dinner out, then *verify* the details: "This is what I want to do to bless you. Is that all right with you?"

The most important *verification* of all is this: Verify with the Lord that your plan is a "God idea," not just a good idea.

There are several other *V*s in servanthood as well:

1. Serve with *vitality*. Be enthusiastic and joyous, even if the person you serve doesn't seem to appreciate it. Sometimes people think they have a right to be served or they just don't appreciate what you are doing. Remember to do everything as unto God, and maintain a godly attitude in your heart. I remember talking with a young man who served as the personal assistant in one of the ministries I visited. I complimented him on his servant heart and said that the servant attitude he reflected blessed me. His response was profound: "It's all well and good being a servant, but when you are being treated like a servant, it's not always easy." Expect to be treated like what you are—*a servant*. False expectations can cause "vitality leaks."

2. When you verify the details of your desire to serve someone, do it very *sensitively*. Never impose your will when you are serving someone. If Jesus never imposes His will over ours, what grounds do we have to impose our will over others?

3. Serve very *cautiously*. Many years ago, long before we knew we would live there, we held a major ministry outreach in Port Elizabeth, South Africa. We sent out 70 people to go from house to house on certain selected streets. From a central base, two prayer warriors backed up each of the 70 ministers in prayer; they interceded for the ministry teams night after night as they ventured out to reach the lost and hurting. On the first night, Carol and I teamed up with a young lady and visited one particular family. I sensed that we should simply love this family and avoid preaching at them that night. The Holy Spirit assured me He would show me *when* to share the gospel. On the final night the Lord said, "This is your night." When I told the family members, "I want to tell you about Jesus," they said, "I wondered when you were going to tell us about Him." God's time is always the right time. That night the whole family surrendered their hearts to Jesus.

4. *Venture out* and don't give in to your fears. The most common excuse I hear for the failure to serve others and reveal the Savior is this: "It's fine for others, but I can't do anything. I'm not creative or educated and I really don't have a lot of resources or talents. What can I do?" I know of an elderly woman of prayer who was uneducated and nearly illiterate. Nevertheless, she loved the Lord and had a burning desire to see her neighborhood receive Jesus Christ. One day she baked a cake and knocked on her neighbor's door. When she announced, "I've come to have a cup of coffee and visit with you; here is a cake," the neighbors were somewhat startled; but they invited her in anyway. As they shared the cake and talked, this lady led her neighbors to the Lord. She did the same thing at every house in her neighborhood. Over a period of months, she led the majority of the people in her suburb to Christ! God has given you a way to serve, no matter who you are or what you can do. Don't be afraid—*venture out*.

Day 5: The Letter *A* in "Servant"

The letter *a* in "servant" reminds us to always **act in love**. This is the day when you *do* what you have prepared for. Do it joyfully. Make it fun for yourself and for the person you are serving if possible. My friend Roddy, who accompanied me to Haiti and on other missions, married a delightful woman who serves as the worship leader in their church. On their wedding day, the wedding guests decided to bless the newlyweds in a hilarious but *loving* way.

During the reception, some of the guests "kidnapped" Roddy's bride and whisked her out of the main reception area. Then they asked him, "Would you like your bride back?" When he predictably replied, "Very much!" they explained that he would have to "ransom" her in a specific way.

Roddy had to go to each table on his hands and knees and beg for ransom money from the guests. The faithful groom pleaded for help and eventually brought the ransom to the kidnappers. When they counted the ransom, they told the anxious groom, "No, that's not enough! Go again!"

Painstakingly and hilariously, poor Roddy went begging from table to table once again. This went on three times until a ransom of several thousand dollars had been collected. This time the kidnappers agreed the ransom total was enough; then they informed Roddy that he could *keep* the ransom money, and they joyfully returned his bride.

You Can Act in Love and Have Fun at the Same Time

The ingenious guests knew that Roddy and his bride had good senses of humor and would not be offended. They managed to bless Roddy and his bride while providing an unforgettable memory that brings joy and laughter to this day whenever it is mentioned. You can *act in love* and have fun at the same time because servanthood is a dignity and a delight.

Many times we must *act in love* even when it isn't fun. Servanthood is always a joy, a dignity and a delight; *but it isn't always easy.* Occasionally the Lord calls us to provide an act of service when it isn't convenient or comfortable.

During our ministry travels over the years, God has often allowed us to pray for the sick. We have witnessed some of the most amazing miracles at these times, but we knew we had to serve whether our prayers for healing were answered at that moment or not. Our greatest test was just around the corner.

One night Carol and I drove some distance from the spot where I was walking on the road with the cross and bowl, to one of South Africa's east-coast city airports to catch a late-night flight to Durban. I was scheduled to hold a series of outreach meetings with several churches that weekend. Before the flight, we phoned our children, who were staying with Carol's parents in Johannesburg.

While Carol talked with our daughter, Carynne, she sensed an urgency in Carynne's voice as she said, "Mommy, Granny is very ill. I know she won't tell you because she doesn't want to alarm you; but please, Mommy, you must come."

Carol knew instantly that Carynne was serious, and she also knew that her parents would do anything to avoid placing us under any pressure or concern. What were we to do? We had the tickets booked, it was 11:00 P.M. and our plane was due to leave for Durban in 25 minutes.

Finally we decided that Carol would fly to Durban as planned and spend the night there. But early the next morning we would put her on the first flight to Johannesburg.

Carol's Mother Was to Be Hospitalized

The following day, by God's grace, Carol boarded a flight to Johannesburg while I stayed in Durban to continue with the hectic weekend schedule. On Monday, I called Carol and she told me her mother was to be hospitalized. Later on she told me her mother was scheduled for exploratory surgery and asked if I would come to Johannesburg.

The next day, Mom went in for surgery; the surgeon returned with bad news. He told my dear wife and her family that Mom had terminal cancer and there was nothing they could do for her. The cancer was too advanced for treatment with chemotherapy. By his estimate, she had between three months and a year to live.

The family was stunned. We tried to rise up in faith at the same time we were reeling from shock. The questions flowed from us with seemingly few answers. "Why, Lord, when she is so young? What could it be? Why should this happen?"

After we shared the grim news with Carol's mom, I knew it was time to return to the road. Carol wanted to get her mom back home and settled in before she rejoined me on the road, which she hoped would take only a few days. It was not to be.

Ten days later, a local pastor came to the trailer with an urgent message for me to call Carol. I rushed to the nearest telephone. With a quivering voice, Carol said that I needed to come to Johannesburg quickly. The doctor didn't expect Carol's mother to make it through the night. After a fast-paced three-hour drive to the nearest airport, I caught a 1:00 A.M. flight and arrived in Johannesburg two hours later.

I walked into Mom's room and saw the whole family gathered there, including Carol's brother and sisters and their spouses. I was shocked to see how much Mom had deteriorated in just 15 days.

We Kept Serving Mom, Even When She Lapsed into a Coma

Carol and I decided to *serve* Mom the best that we could while she still had breath in her. I got up every morning and sat at Mom's bedside. All day long, hour after hour, I read or spoke the Word of God to her. This went on from sunrise to sunset, and then Carol would take over. She sat with her mom throughout the night, praying, bathing and keeping vigil at her bedside. We kept doing these things, even when she lapsed into a coma.

Five days later we could see the end was near, and I said to her, "Mom, do you see Jesus coming for you? He's coming for you. Just reach out your arms and step into His"—and she did.

Imagine what a revival of servanthood would do to your church and community! People would begin to say, "We know about them! We know all about their kindness!"

The long hours we spent at the bedside of one we loved so dearly marked one of our hardest battles in life. At times we cried out to God in pain as we served Carol's dying mother, but with deep dignity we were able to serve her until she stepped into the arms of Jesus. At times, *the Lord simply calls us to be available to serve.* Even though it won't always be easy, serve with dignity and delight.

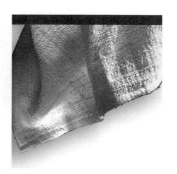

Day 6: The Letter *N* in "Servant"

The letter *n* in the word "servant" signifies our call to serve others for **nothing in return**. This is the day we spend in prayer. By this I mean, simply thank God all day long. Thank Him for the privilege of being used for His glory. As we thank Him, we ask for nothing in return. Simply say, "God, I *expect nothing in return*. It is such an honor to be Your servant." Servants have no rights. Give up your "right" to complain and to be treated with respect. Christ served and was crucified—*some thanks He received!* Expect ingratitude and thanklessness. You are a servant. Take your joy from His presence and you will find strength sufficient for the day. Let your heart overflow with gratitude and joy throughout the day. Worship and praise the Lord for choosing to extend to you the privilege of the high calling to be His *servant*.

Day 7: The Letter *T* in "Servant"

The letter *t* in "servant" signifies the day we set aside to **tarry,** or wait, on the Lord. That is the day we ask the Lord to show us whom we should serve the following week (it could be an individual, a couple or a family) and what step to take next.

If you serve one individual or one family for a week, by the end of the year you will have served 52 different individuals or families. Multiply that number by the number of Christians in your home church to estimate how many thousands of people could be served in your community *if . . .*

This should give you a glimpse of what can happen *if the spirit of serving truly breaks out* and your entire church puts down the sword and picks up the towel of servanthood.

Even the mere possibility of what can be causes my heart to leap for joy. *Imagine what a revival of servanthood would do to your church and community!* Wouldn't it be great to live in "the community that loves" and attend "the church that serves"? People would begin to say, "We know about them! We know all about their kindness. Everyone in that church serves!"

Revival always begins in the heart and spreads one heart at a time. Don't wait for others to capture the vision. Dare to take the lead as a follower and servant of Christ. Allow the Lord to change your "spiritual DNA" and make servanthood *something that you are*, not *something that you do*. Jesus said that if you want to be great in His kingdom, you must be a servant. *This is the secret to greatness.*

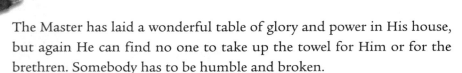

The Master has laid a wonderful table of glory and power in His house, but again He can find no one to take up the towel for Him or for the brethren. Somebody has to be humble and broken.

Somebody—anybody—who can weep enough tears to wash filthy feet will have a place of honor reserved at the side of our Servant leader. He made of Himself no reputation, but we constantly attempt to build ours. He took upon Himself the form of a servant while we try to make ourselves lords.[9]

Many of us would be willing to wash *His* feet, but He demands that if we would wash His feet, then we *must* wash others' feet as well. The King of glory seeks shoe-shining servants for His court and kingdom. The time for study, discussion and pondering is over. Now it is time to act.

He summons His kingdom of kings and priests to lay down their crowns and take up their towels of humble servitude in His name. "But whoever desires to become great among you, let him be your servant."[10]

The towel seems like a limp and lifeless symbol to a Church enamored with vibrant speakers and flashy gifts; but *towels wielded properly build His kingdom faster than swords wielded improperly.* Let's get it right.

For too long we've used the right weapon in the wrong realm. The cutting edge of the sword is for the devil and the obstacles he erects to block our way. It is the harvest season, when the Master needs servants in the wheat fields. Reserve your sword for the spiritual battles and look to the fields. It is time to pick up your towel and reap the harvest.

Notes
  1. James 2:20.
  2. Hebrews 12:1-3.
  3. Psalm 46:10, italics mine.
  4. See John 21:2,3.
  5. John 21:5,6,9,10,12, italics mine.
  6. See Luke 10:34.
  7. Luke 10:35.
  8. Revelation 19:10.
  9. See Philippians 2:7.
 10. Matthew 20:26.

IF YOU WISH TO CONTACT

DAVID CAPE,

PLEASE USE ONE OF THE

FOLLOWING ADDRESSES:

FOOTWASHER MINISTRIES

United States:
P.O. Box 9416, Richmond, VA
23228-0416

Republic of South Africa:
P.O. Box 13854, Humewood, Port Elizabeth
6013 Rep. of South Africa

E-mail: info@footwasher.net

PURSUING HIS PRESENCE

(audiotape album) $20 plus $3 S&H

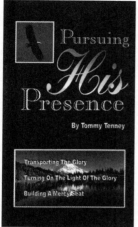

Tape 1 - Transporting the Glory: The only thing that can carry "the ark" (the glory of God) is sanctification, the developing of godly character. Also learn about "divine radiation zones" and hear an exciting testimony about a man's crushed hand that was miraculously healed, the repercussions of which affected his entire town!

Tape 2 - Turning On the Light of the Glory: This best-selling tape has literally gone around the world. Tommy deals with turning on the light of the glory and presence of God, and he walks us through the necessary process and ingredients to potentially unleash what His Body has always dreamed of—God dwelling in the Church to such a measure that there comes a great visitation of His presence to bring revival in the land.

Tape 3 - Building a Mercy Seat: If we build the mercy seat—in the spiritual sense—according to the pattern that God gave to Moses, the same thing will happen as occurred when the original was built. The presence of God came and dwelt between the out-stretched wings of the worshiping cherubim. In worshiping, we create an appropriate environment in which the presence of God can dwell, which was the whole focus of the Old Testament tabernacle.

FANNING THE FLAMES

(audiotape album) $20 plus $3 S&H

Tape 1 - The Application of the Blood and the Ark of the Covenant: Most of the churches in America today dwell in an outer-court experience. God said He would dwell in the mercy seat. Jesus' death and sacrifice paralleled the sacri-fice of the high priest who entered behind the veil to make atonement with the blood of animals. Jesus made atone-ment with His own blood, once for all, and the veil in the temple was rent from top to bottom.

Tape 2 - A Tale of Two Cities—Nazareth & Ninevah: In this challenging message, Tommy contrasts Nazareth with Ninevah. Jesus spent more time in Nazareth than any other city, yet there was great resistance to the works of God there. A haughty spirit, arrogance, and unbelief are not fer-tile ground for the Lord to move. In contrast, consider the characteristics of the people of Ninevah.

Tape 3 - The "I" Factor: Examine the difference between *ikabod* and *kabod* ("glory"). The arm of flesh cannot achieve what needs to be done. God doesn't need us; we need Him. Our churches have been filled with noise, but devoid of worship. Real worship only comes from those who are willing to stand in the gap. Let the axe be laid to the root of the tree when it comes to religious spirits.

1. Fear Not
2. Hanging In There
3. Fire of God

There is a swelling tide of hunger for spiritual things sweeping through the world. We call for His fire to come, but we have to be touched by the baptism of fire before we can be a fire breather.

KEYS TO LIVING THE REVIVED LIFE
(audiotape album) $20 plus $3 S&H

Tape 1 - Fear Not: Fear is faith in reverse. Whatever faith accomplishes by progress, fear accomplishes by regression. The principles that Tommy reveals teach us that to have no fear is to have faith, and that perfect love casts out fear, so we establish the trust of a child in our loving Father. The Scriptures are replete with examples of heavenly messengers beginning their message with these two significant words, "Fear not." Obviously, it is a message from heaven for earth.

Tape 2 - Hanging In There: Have you ever been tempted to give up, quit, and throw in the towel? This message is a word of encouragement for you. Everybody has a place and a position in the Kingdom of God. Any of us can be as great as the most anointed teachers, pastors, and gifted men and women, because of one extremely important criterion for being a hero that often goes overlooked. Jeannie Tenney joins her husband and sings an inspiring chorus, "I'm going through."

Tape 3 - Fire of God: Fire purges the sewer of our souls and destroys the hidden things that would cause disease. Fire perfects our praise. How does a church living, for the most part, powerless, in defeat and shackled by shame, become free and walk in victory? Learn the way out of a repetitive cycle of seasonal times of failure. When the church becomes a place where people can expose their withered crippledness, healing will take place.

DYNAMIC CHRISTIAN LIVING
(audiotape album), $20 plus $3 S&H

Tape 1 - Preserving the Family: This manifesto on the unsurpassed importance of preserving the integrity of the family unit highlights God's desire to heal the wounds of dysfunctional families, from the inside out.

Tape 2 - Unity in the Body: Despite the abuse of the term *unity*, godly unity in truth is a priority on our Father's heart. Tommy examines four levels of unity that must be respected and achieved before we will see the true unity that is so needed in the Body.

Tape 3 - Dealing With Rejection: No one has known continual rejection as much as Jesus did. As followers of Jesus, we know we will be despised and rejected. Here is concrete help in dealing victoriously with rejection and the life-sapping emotions that can result.

Tommy Tenney

1. Preserving The Family
2. Unity In The Body
3. Dealing With Rejection

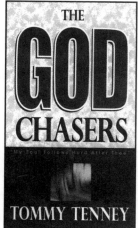

THE GOD CHASERS, VOLUME 1
(audiotape album) $20 plus $3 S&H

These are the foundational tapes for the best-selling book, *The God Chasers*, by Tommy Tenney.

Tape 1 - Seeking God's Agenda—The Road to Revival: Recounts a dramatic present-day intervention of God in a service where a pulpit was split at Christian Tabernacle in Houston, Texas. Now is a time to seek God's face (His presence) and not His hand (His benefits).

Tape 2 - The Holiness of the Ark of God: We have tried long enough to usher in the presence of God "our way." It is now time to do so God's way. We need to learn how to revere His sacred presence.

Tape 3 - The Bread of His Presence: "Revival does not occur because people seek revival. Revival occurs when we seek Him." The presence of God is something that we should carry with us, such that it touches people around us, wherever we are.

TURNING ON THE LIGHT OF THE GLORY
(video) $19 plus $2 S&H

This best-selling message has literally gone around the world. Tommy deals with turning on the light of the glory and presence of God, and he walks us through the necessary process and ingredients to potentially unleash what His Body has always dreamed of—God dwelling in the Church to such a measure that there comes a great visitation of His presence to bring revival in the land.

Best-Sellers from Regal

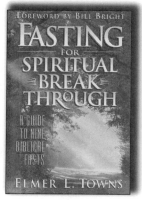
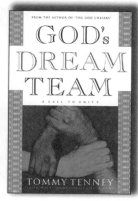
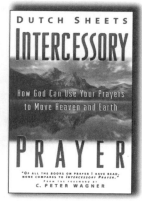

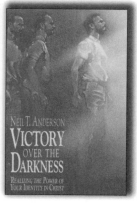
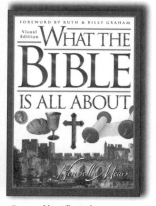